W9-ATD-380

GRAPHIC LIBRARY

GRAPHIC HISTORY

THE STORY OF Jamestown

by Eric Braun
illustrated by Steve Erwin,
Keith Williams, and Charles Barnett III

Consultant:
Crandall A. Shifflett, Professor of History
Virginia Tech
Blacksburg, Virginia

Capstone press
Mankato, Minnesota

Graphic Library is published by Capstone Press,
151 Good Counsel Drive, P.O. Box 669, Mankato, Minnesota 56002.
www.capstonepress.com

Printed in the United States of America

1 2 3 4 5 6 10 09 08 07 06 05

Library of Congress Cataloging-in-Publication Data
Braun, Eric, 1971–
The story of Jamestown / by Eric Braun; illustrated by Steve Erwin, Keith Williams, and Charles Barnett III.
p. cm.—(Graphic library. Graphic history)
Includes bibliographical references and index.
ISBN 0-7368-4967-X (hardcover)
1. Jamestown (Va.)—History—Juvenile literature. I. Erwin, Steve, ill. II. Williams, Keith, ill. III. Barnett, Charles, III, ill. IV. Title. V. Series.
F234.J3B69 2006
975.5'4251—dc22 2005013592

Summary: In graphic novel format, tells the story of Jamestown, the first permanent English settlement in North America.

Art and Editorial Direction
Jason Knudson and Blake A. Hoena

Designers
Bob Lentz and Juliette Peters

Colorist
Ben Hunzeker

Editor
Donald Lemke

Editor's note: Direct quotations from primary sources are indicated by a yellow background.

Direct quotations appear on the following pages:
Pages 17, 25 (all), from *Love and Hate in Jamestown: John Smith, Pocahontas, and the Heart of a New Nation* by David A. Price (New York: Knopf, 2003).

Table of Contents

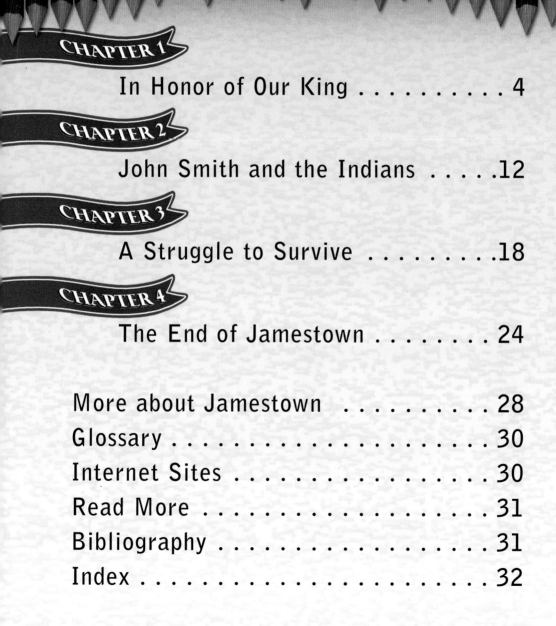

CHAPTER 1

In Honor of Our King

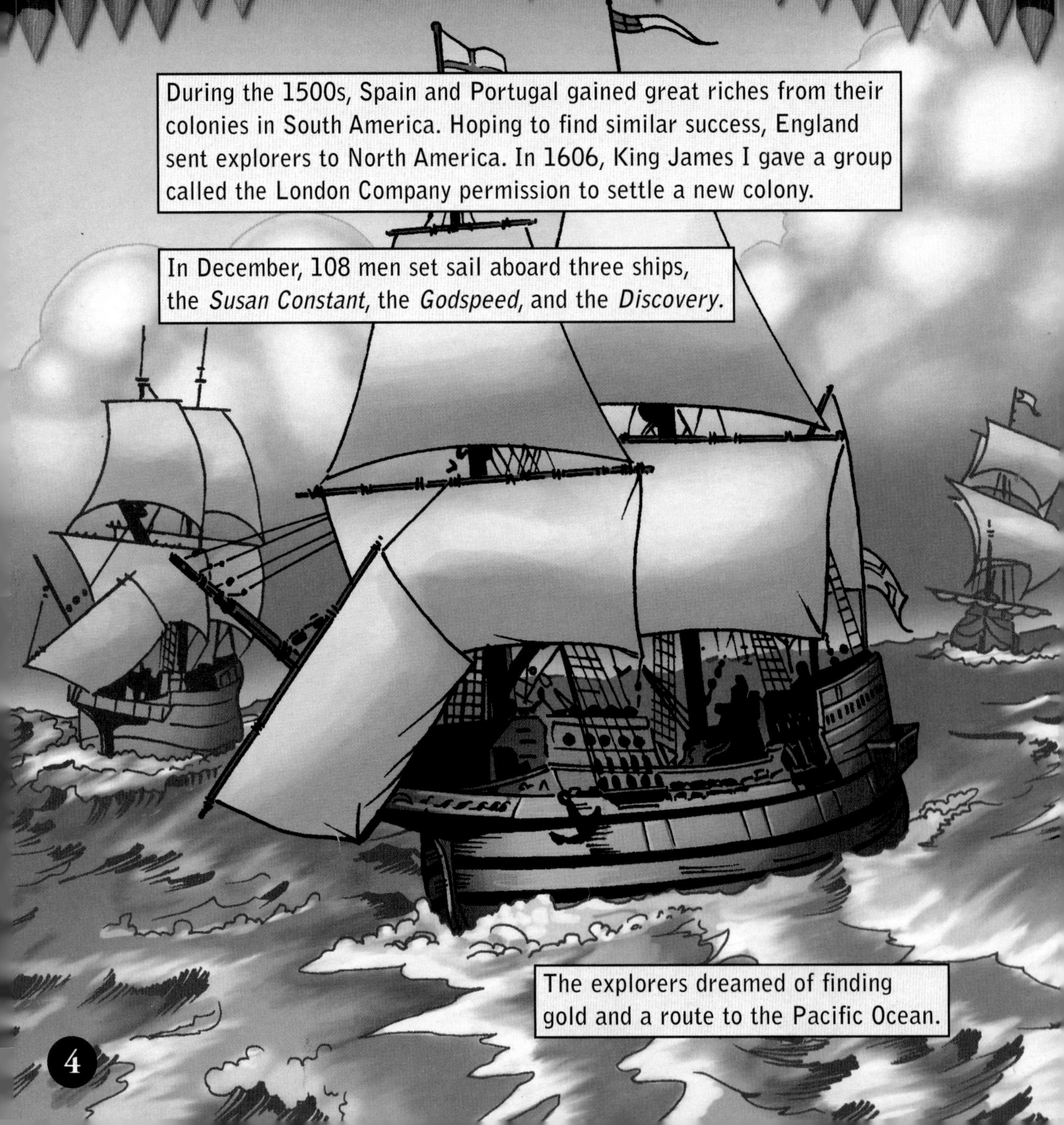

During the 1500s, Spain and Portugal gained great riches from their colonies in South America. Hoping to find similar success, England sent explorers to North America. In 1606, King James I gave a group called the London Company permission to settle a new colony.
In December, 108 men set sail aboard three ships, the *Susan Constant*, the *Godspeed*, and the *Discovery*.
The explorers dreamed of finding gold and a route to the Pacific Ocean.

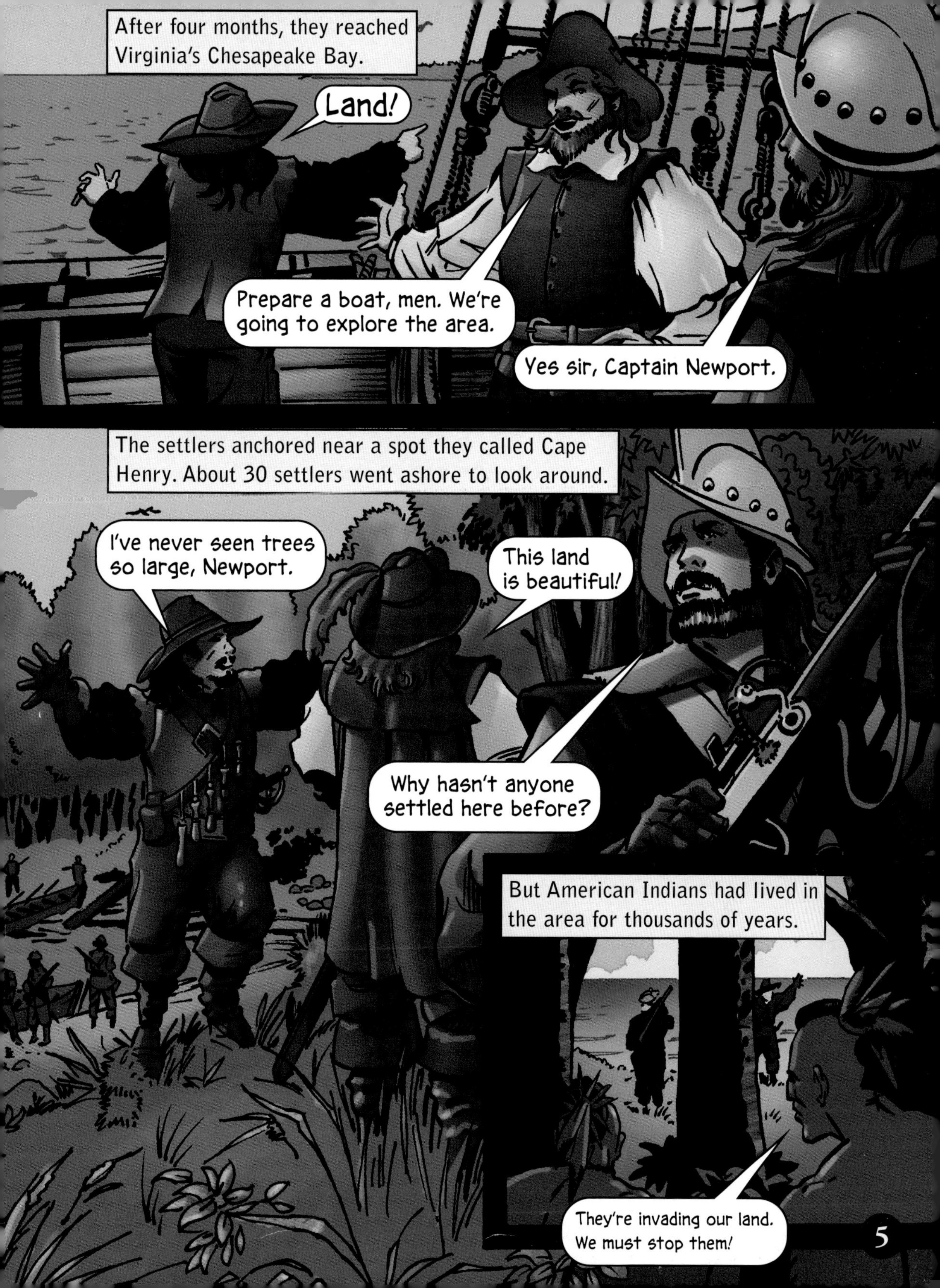
After four months, they reached Virginia's Chesapeake Bay.
Land!
Prepare a boat, men. We're going to explore the area.
Yes sir, Captain Newport.
The settlers anchored near a spot they called Cape Henry. About 30 settlers went ashore to look around.
I've never seen trees so large, Newport.
This land is beautiful!
Why hasn't anyone settled here before?
But American Indians had lived in the area for thousands of years.
They're invading our land. We must stop them!

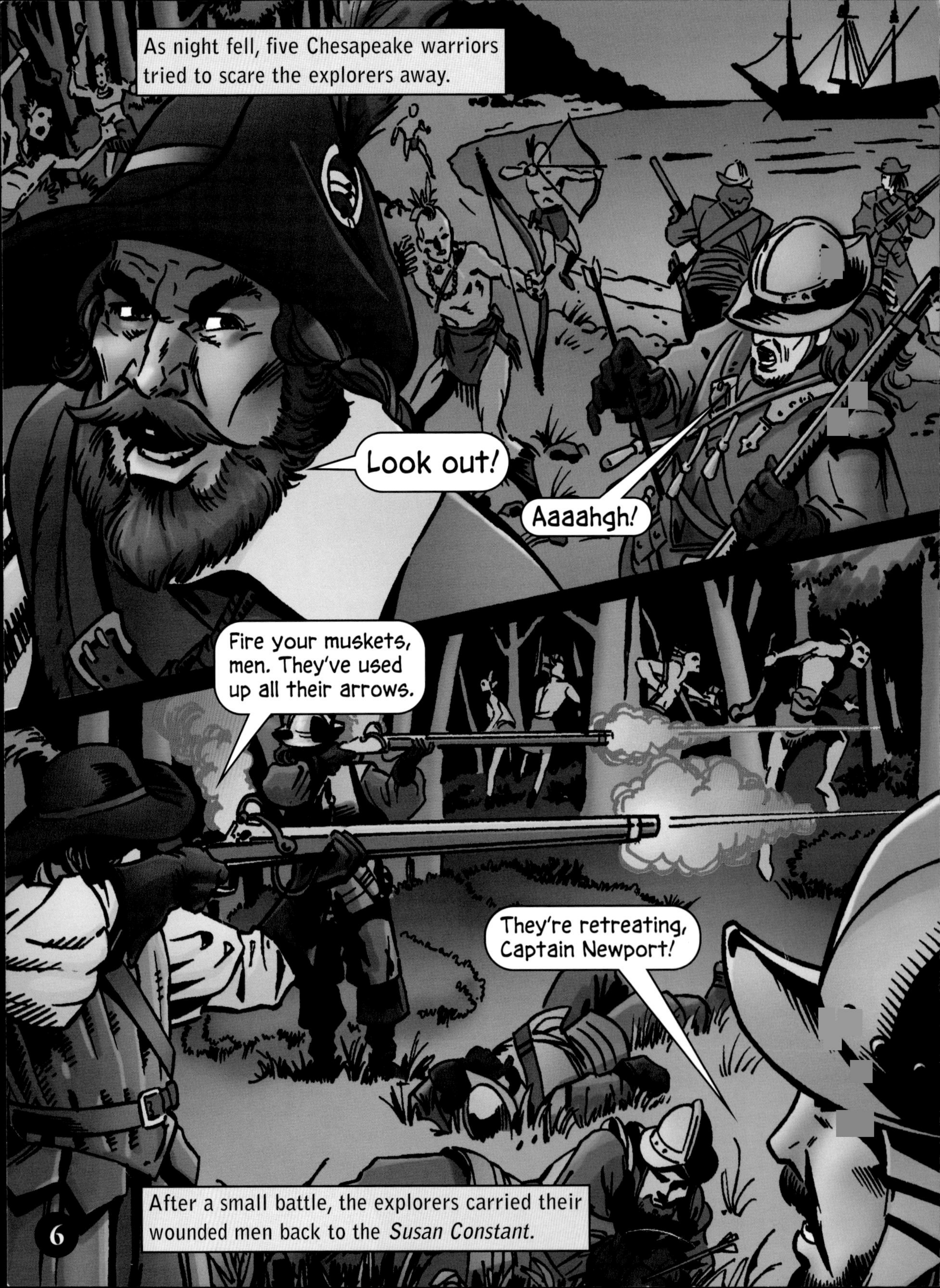
As night fell, five Chesapeake warriors tried to scare the explorers away.
Look out!
Aaaahgh!
Fire your muskets, men. They've used up all their arrows.
They're retreating, Captain Newport!
After a small battle, the explorers carried their wounded men back to the *Susan Constant*.

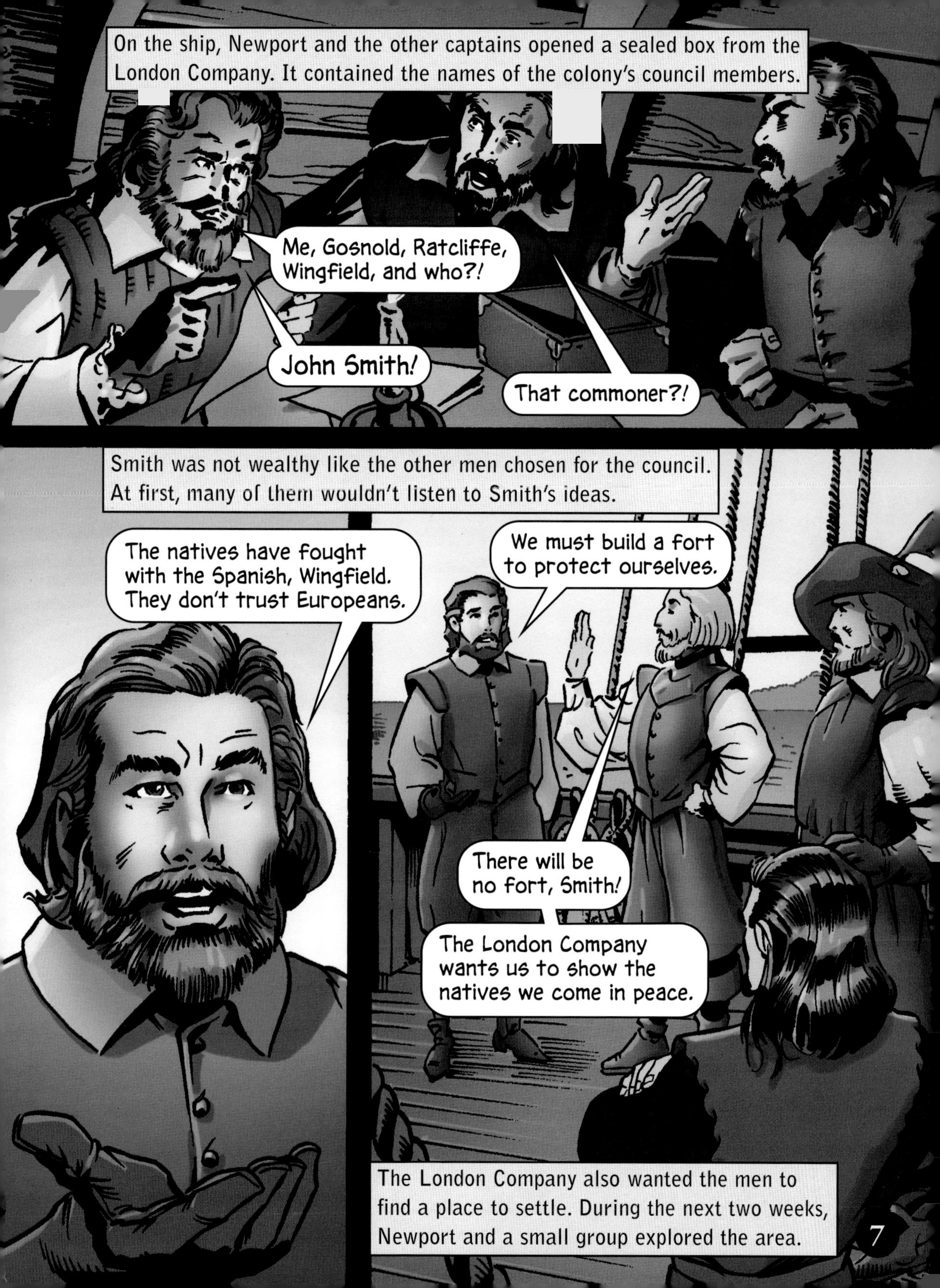
On the ship, Newport and the other captains opened a sealed box from the London Company. It contained the names of the colony's council members.
Me, Gosnold, Ratcliffe, Wingfield, and who?!
John Smith!
That commoner?!
Smith was not wealthy like the other men chosen for the council. At first, many of them wouldn't listen to Smith's ideas.
The natives have fought with the Spanish, Wingfield. They don't trust Europeans.
We must build a fort to protect ourselves.
There will be no fort, Smith!
The London Company wants us to show the natives we come in peace.
The London Company also wanted the men to find a place to settle. During the next two weeks, Newport and a small group explored the area.

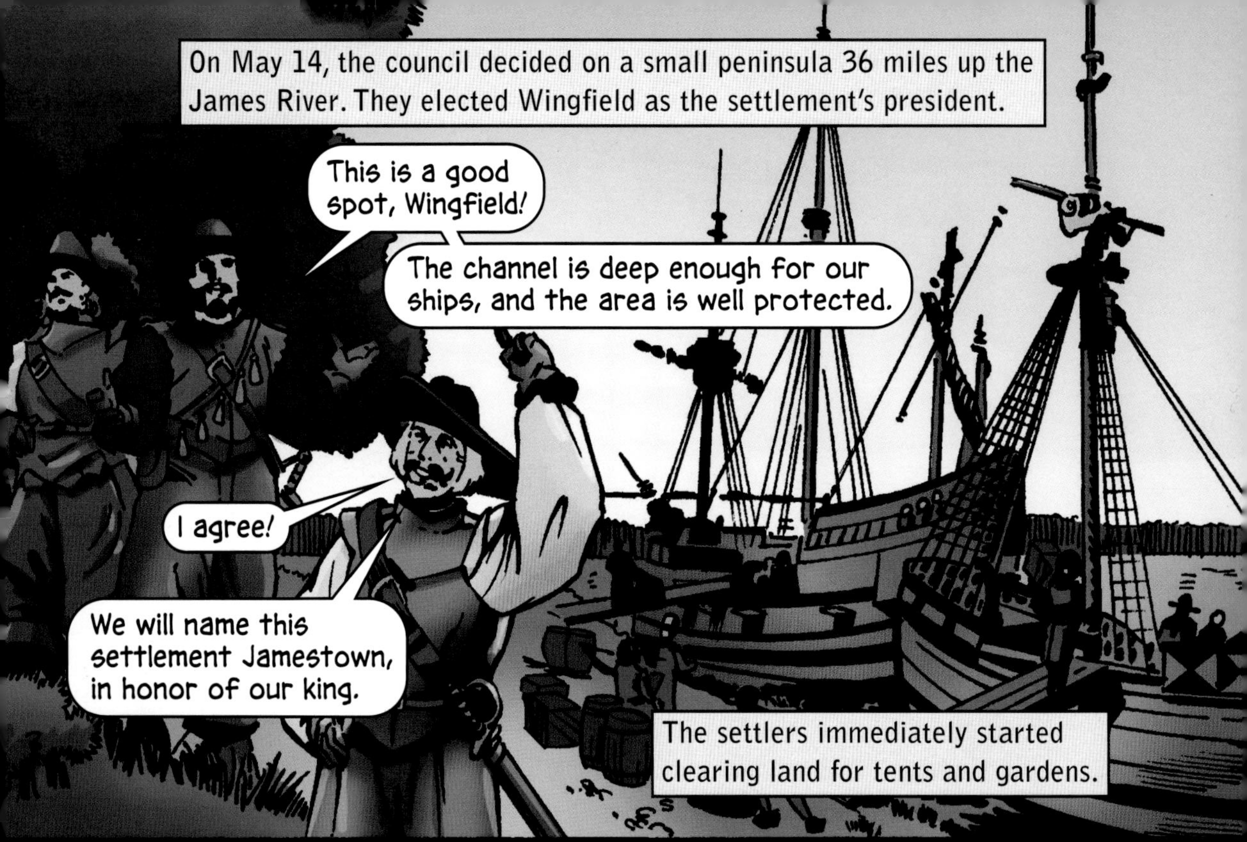
On May 14, the council decided on a small peninsula 36 miles up the James River. They elected Wingfield as the settlement's president.
This is a good spot, Wingfield!
The channel is deep enough for our ships, and the area is well protected.
I agree!
We will name this settlement Jamestown, in honor of our king.
The settlers immediately started clearing land for tents and gardens.

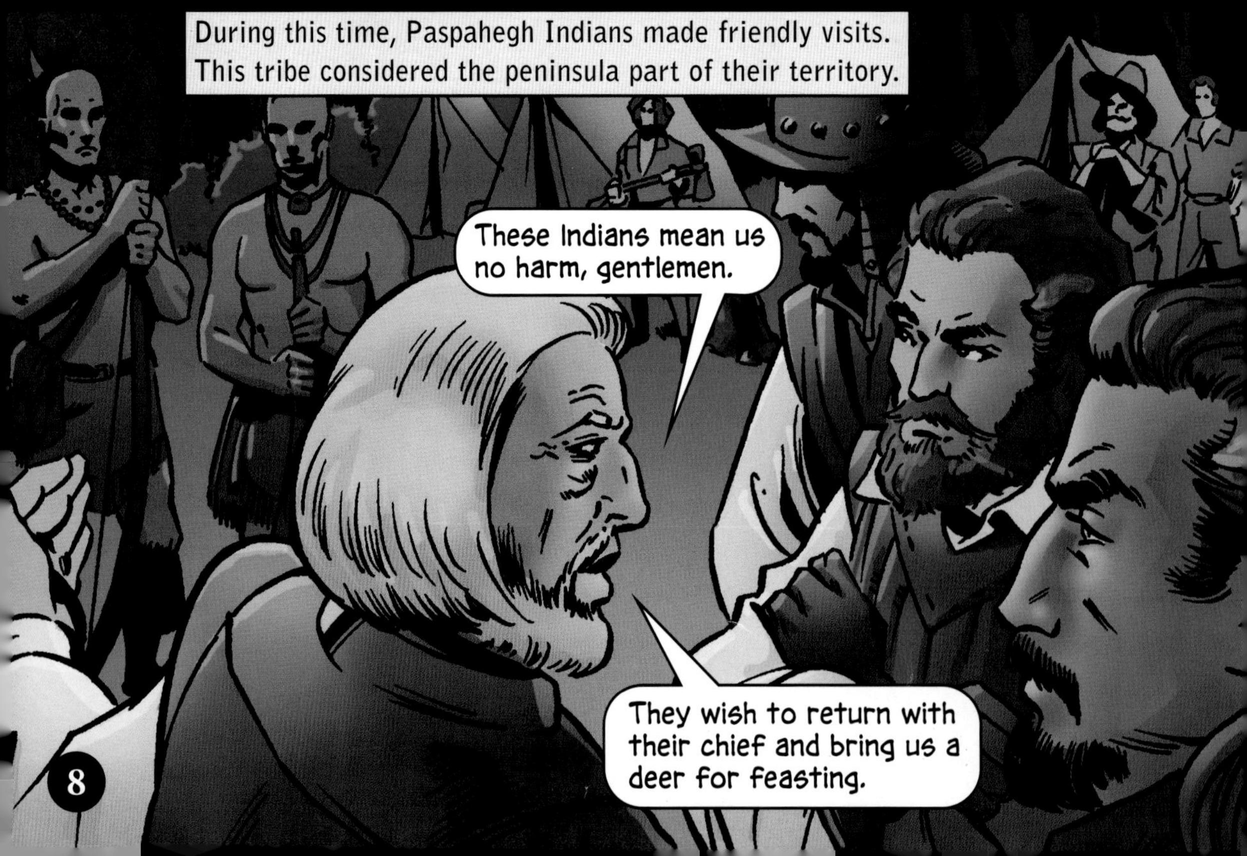
During this time, Paspahegh Indians made friendly visits. This tribe considered the peninsula part of their territory.
These Indians mean us no harm, gentlemen.
They wish to return with their chief and bring us a deer for feasting.

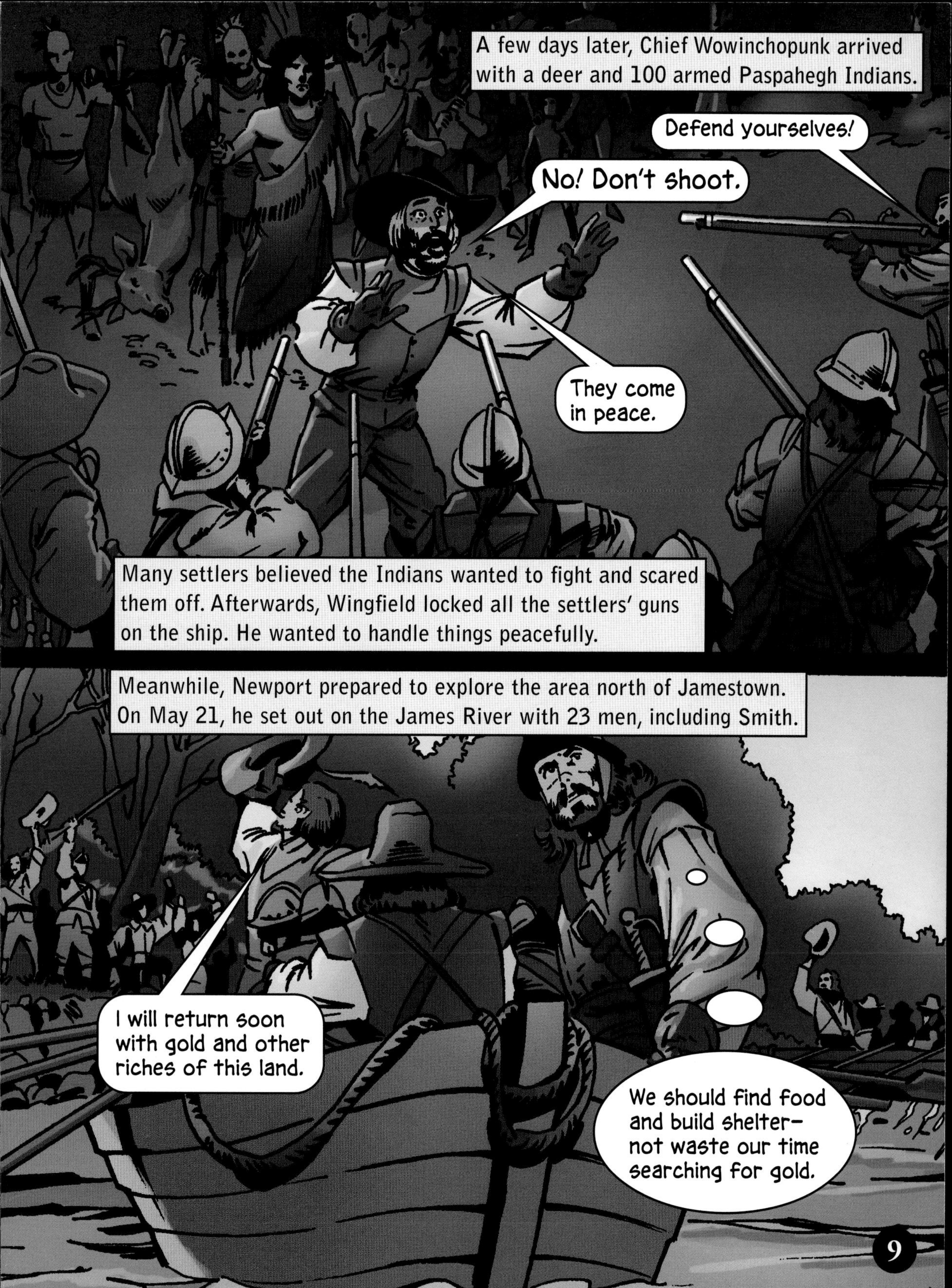
A few days later, Chief Wowinchopunk arrived with a deer and 100 armed Paspahegh Indians.
Defend yourselves!
No! Don't shoot.
They come in peace.
Many settlers believed the Indians wanted to fight and scared them off. Afterwards, Wingfield locked all the settlers' guns on the ship. He wanted to handle things peacefully.
Meanwhile, Newport prepared to explore the area north of Jamestown. On May 21, he set out on the James River with 23 men, including Smith.
I will return soon with gold and other riches of this land.
We should find food and build shelter—not waste our time searching for gold.

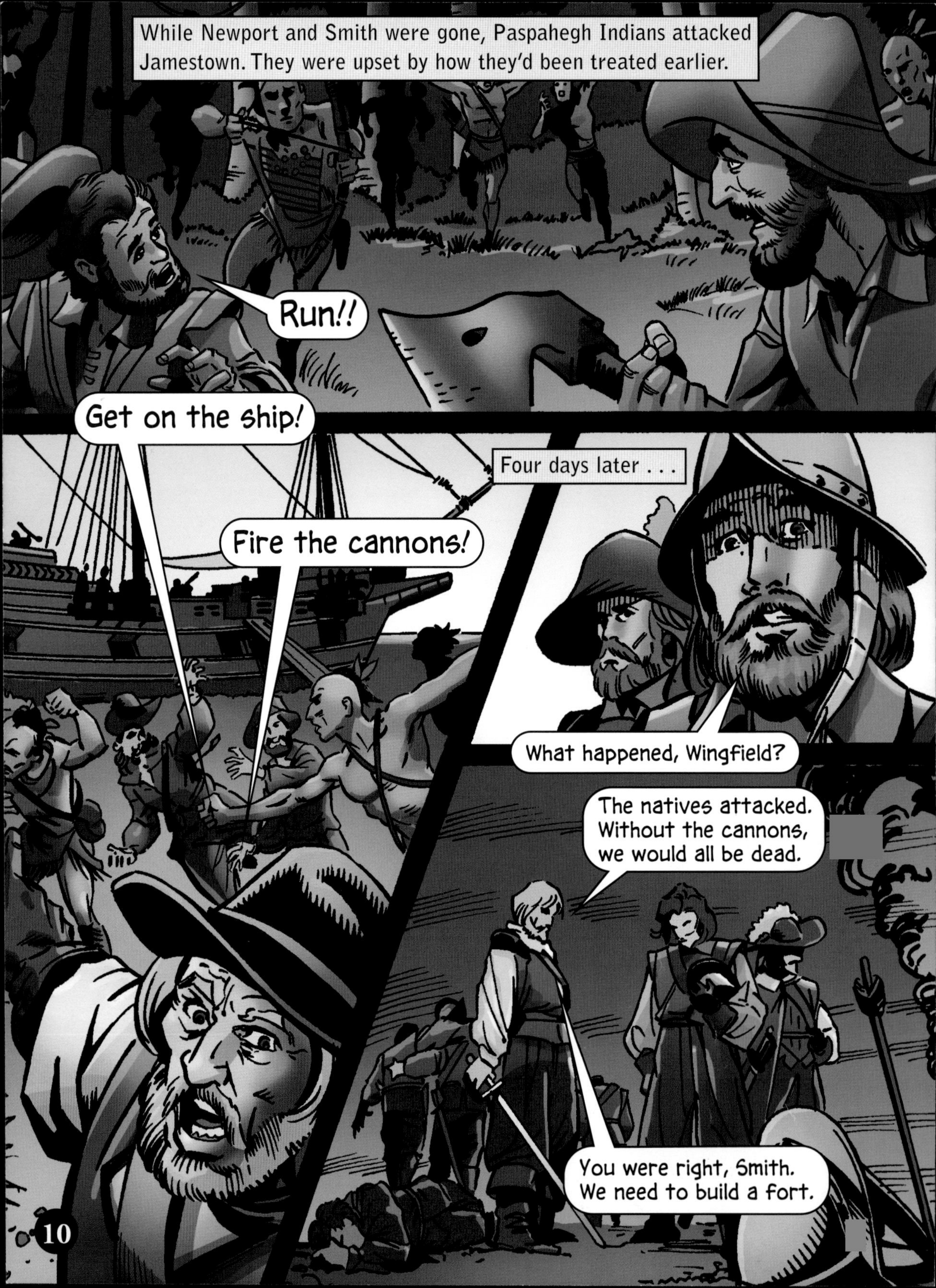
While Newport and Smith were gone, Paspahegh Indians attacked Jamestown. They were upset by how they'd been treated earlier.
Run!!
Get on the ship!
Fire the cannons!
Four days later . . .
What happened, Wingfield?
The natives attacked. Without the cannons, we would all be dead.
You were right, Smith. We need to build a fort.

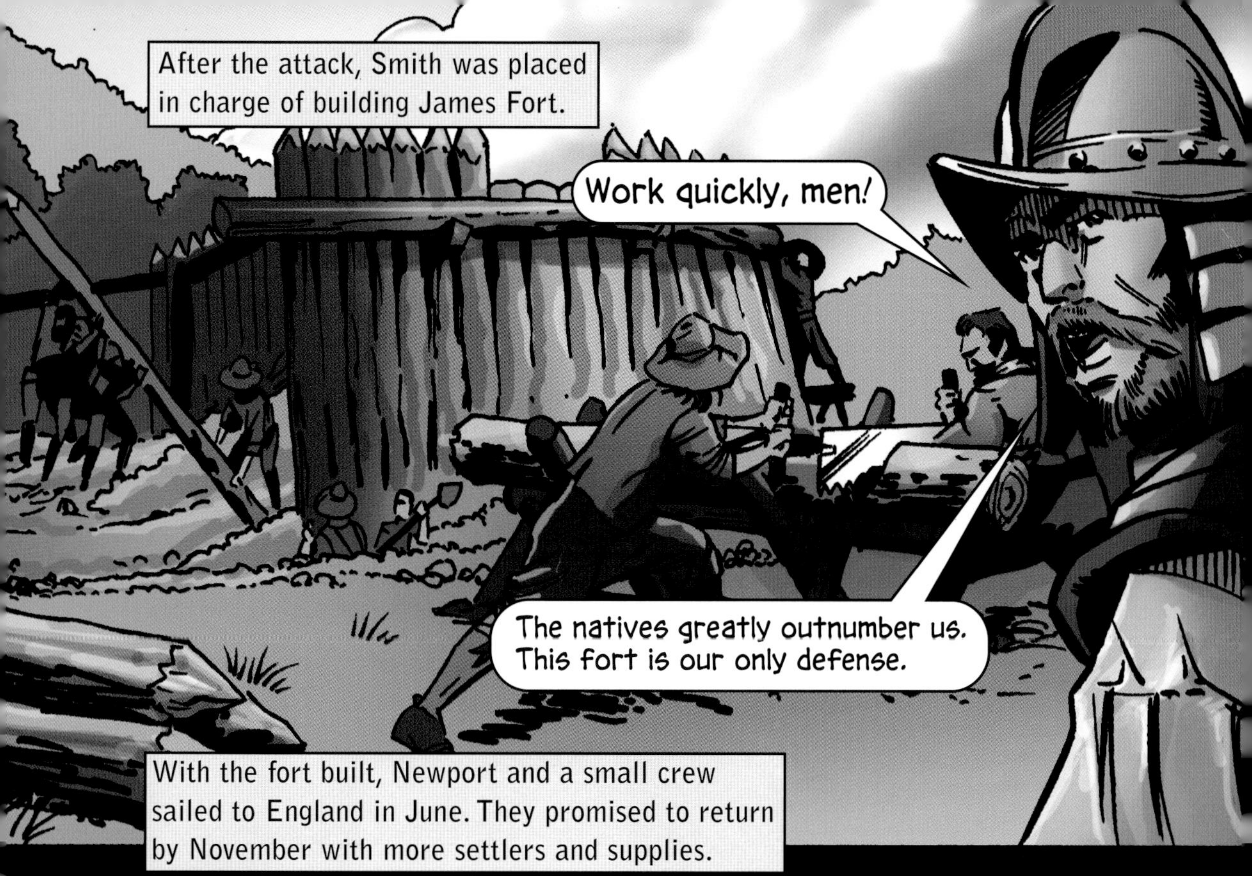
After the attack, Smith was placed in charge of building James Fort.
Work quickly, men!
The natives greatly outnumber us. This fort is our only defense.
With the fort built, Newport and a small crew sailed to England in June. They promised to return by November with more settlers and supplies.

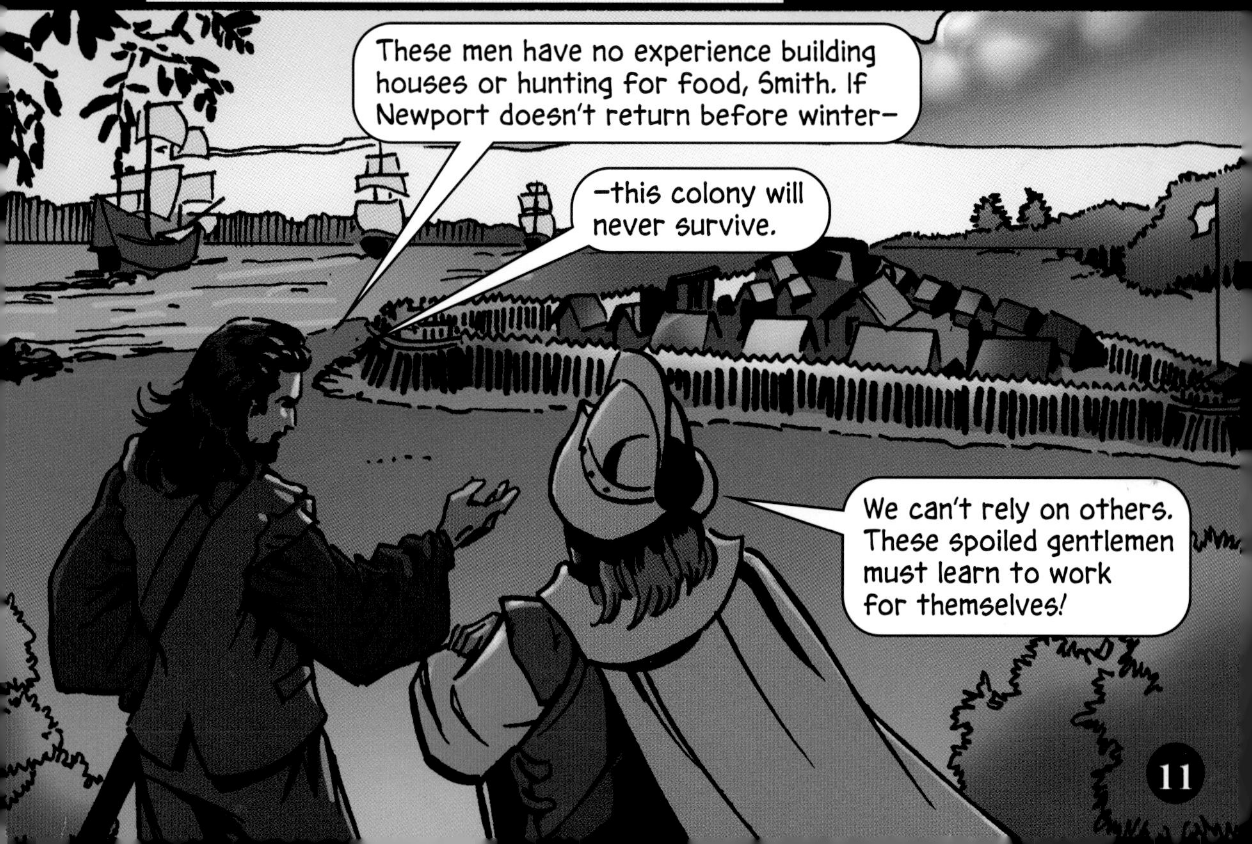
These men have no experience building houses or hunting for food, Smith. If Newport doesn't return before winter—
—this colony will never survive.
We can't rely on others. These spoiled gentlemen must learn to work for themselves!

CHAPTER 2

John Smith and the Indians

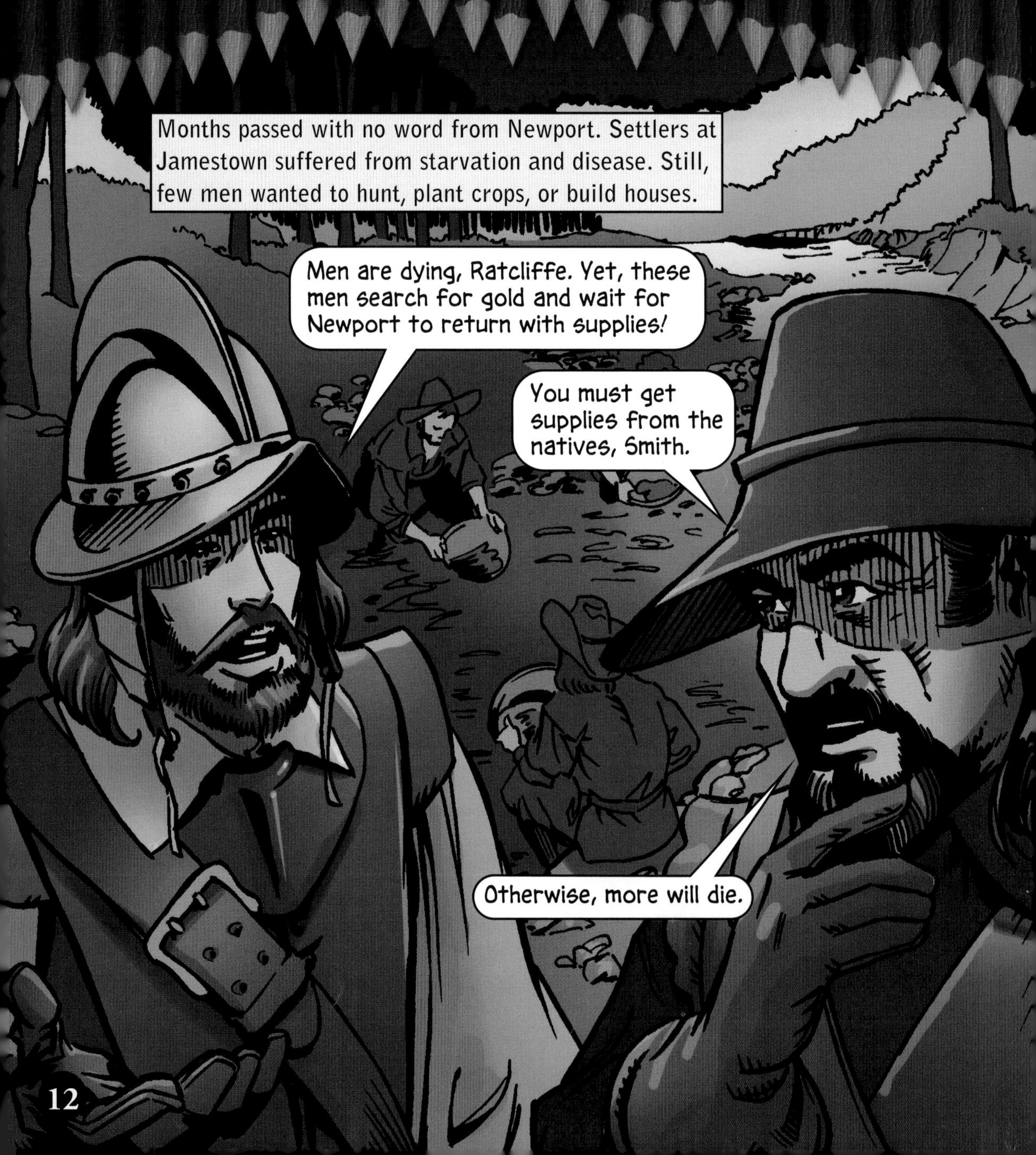

Months passed with no word from Newport. Settlers at Jamestown suffered from starvation and disease. Still, few men wanted to hunt, plant crops, or build houses.
Men are dying, Ratcliffe. Yet, these men search for gold and wait for Newport to return with supplies!
You must get supplies from the natives, Smith.
Otherwise, more will die.

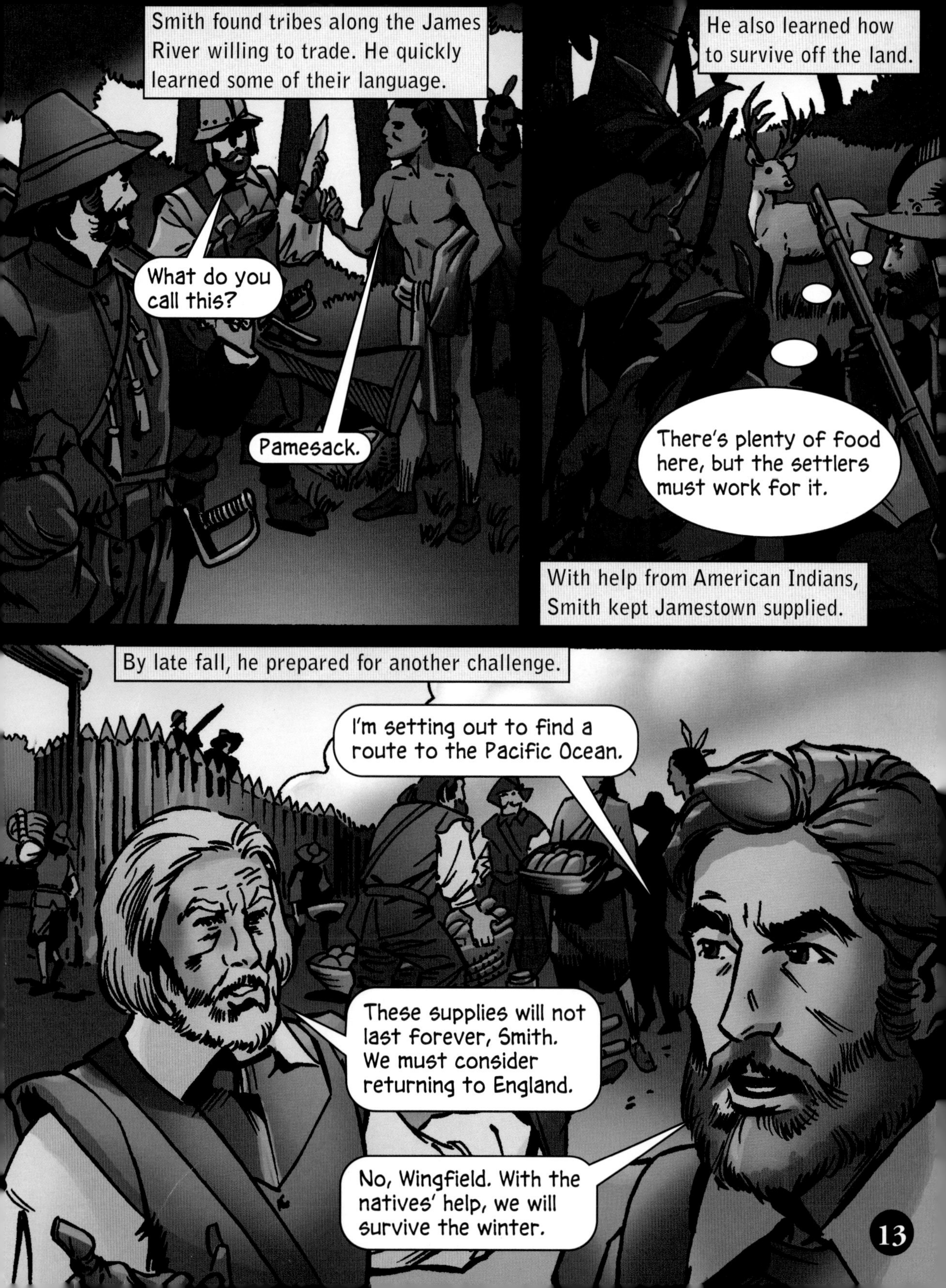

Smith found tribes along the James River willing to trade. He quickly learned some of their language.
What do you call this?
Pamesack.
He also learned how to survive off the land.
There's plenty of food here, but the settlers must work for it.
With help from American Indians, Smith kept Jamestown supplied.
By late fall, he prepared for another challenge.
I'm setting out to find a route to the Pacific Ocean.
These supplies will not last forever, Smith. We must consider returning to England.
No, Wingfield. With the natives' help, we will survive the winter.

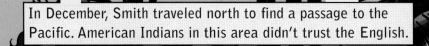

In December, Smith traveled north to find a passage to the Pacific. American Indians in this area didn't trust the English.

Don't kill me. I'm the leader of my people!

I will not harm a leader. My brother, Chief Powhatan, will decide your fate.

Smith learned that Powhatan ruled a group of about 30 tribes in the area. This group was called the Powhatan Confederacy.

We're only here to trade and explore.

I rule this land. The white people cannot stay here.

Then we will leave.

Powhatan and his men didn't know if they could believe Smith.
If the white men truly mean no harm, they could be helpful.
They threaten our empire, Chief. Killing the leader would show them your power.
Do not hurt him, Father!
Smith believed that Powhatan's daughter, Pocahontas, helped her father make a decision.
After two days, the chief released Smith.
You are free to return to your fort. We are friends now.
The chief's daughter has saved my life.

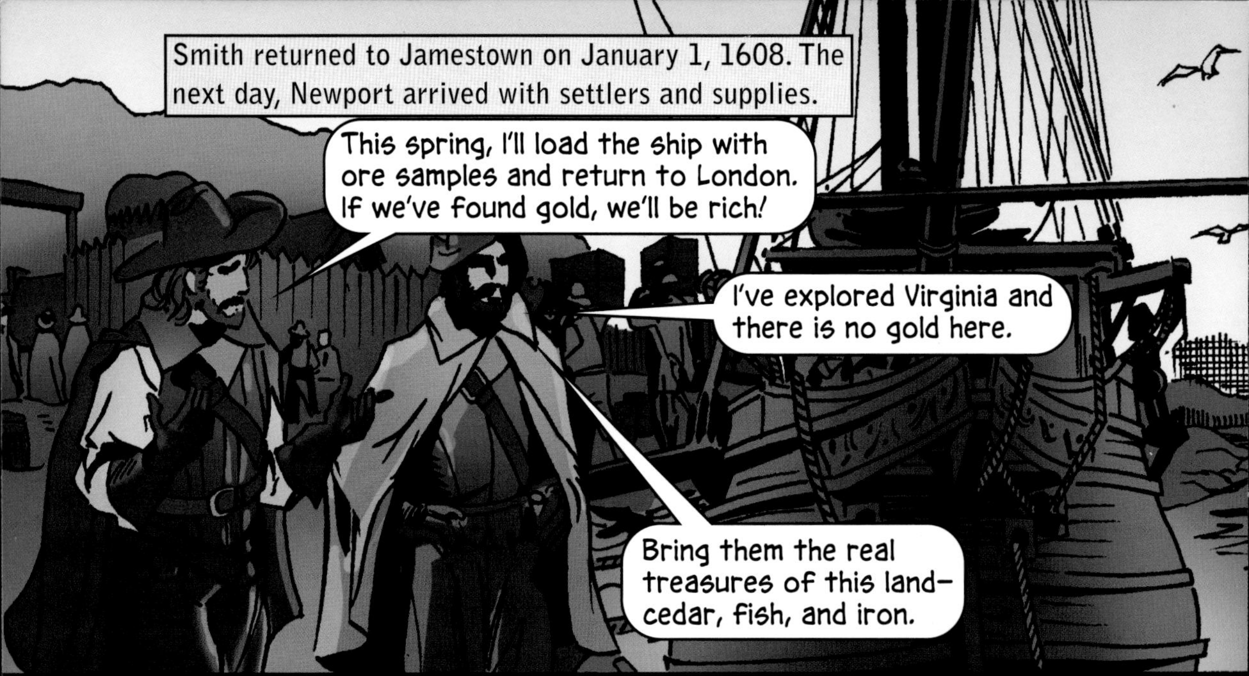
Smith returned to Jamestown on January 1, 1608. The next day, Newport arrived with settlers and supplies.
This spring, I'll load the ship with ore samples and return to London. If we've found gold, we'll be rich!
I've explored Virginia and there is no gold here.
Bring them the real treasures of this land— cedar, fish, and iron.

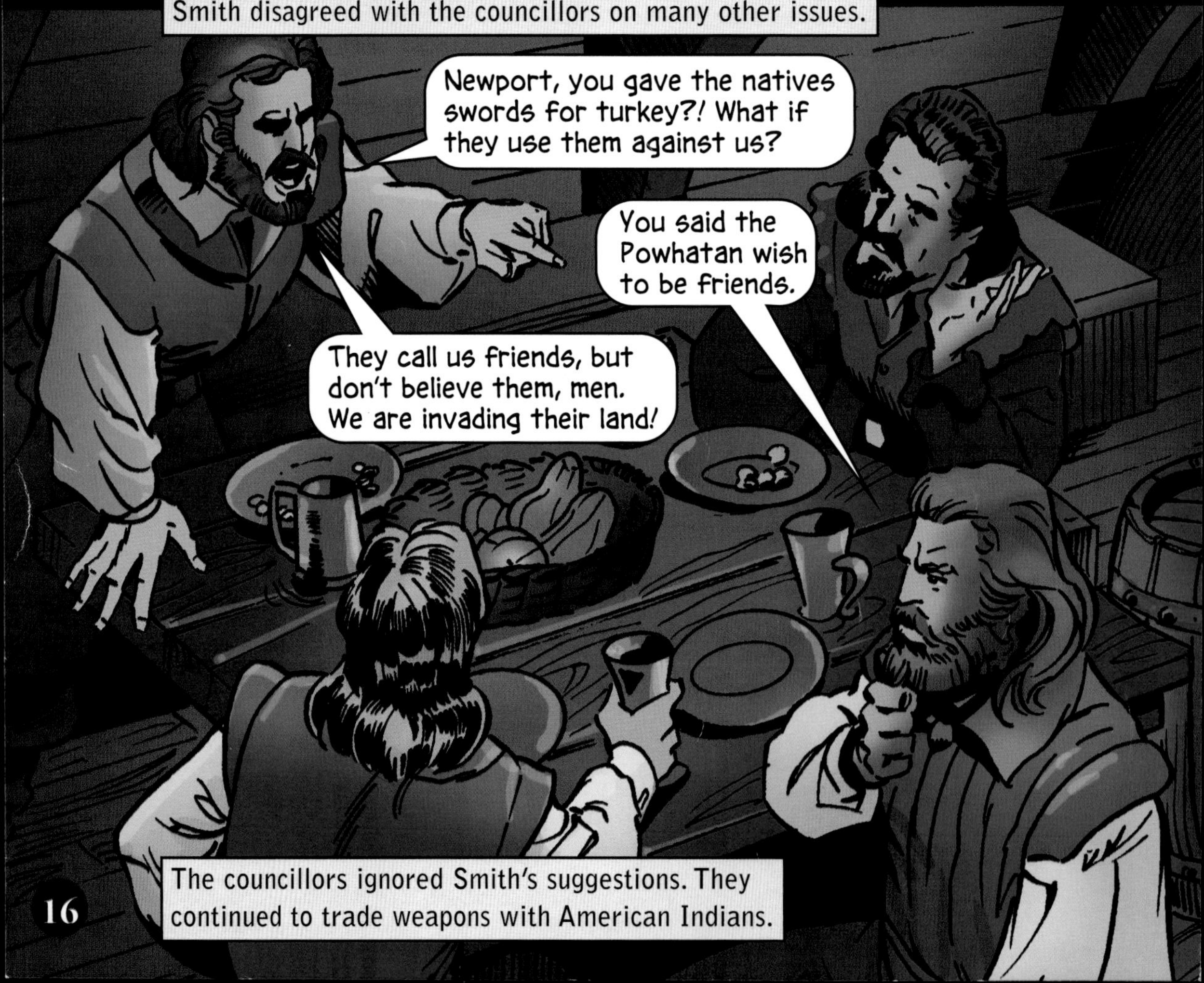
Smith disagreed with the councillors on many other issues.
Newport, you gave the natives swords for turkey?! What if they use them against us?
You said the Powhatan wish to be friends.
They call us friends, but don't believe them, men. We are invading their land!
The councillors ignored Smith's suggestions. They continued to trade weapons with American Indians.

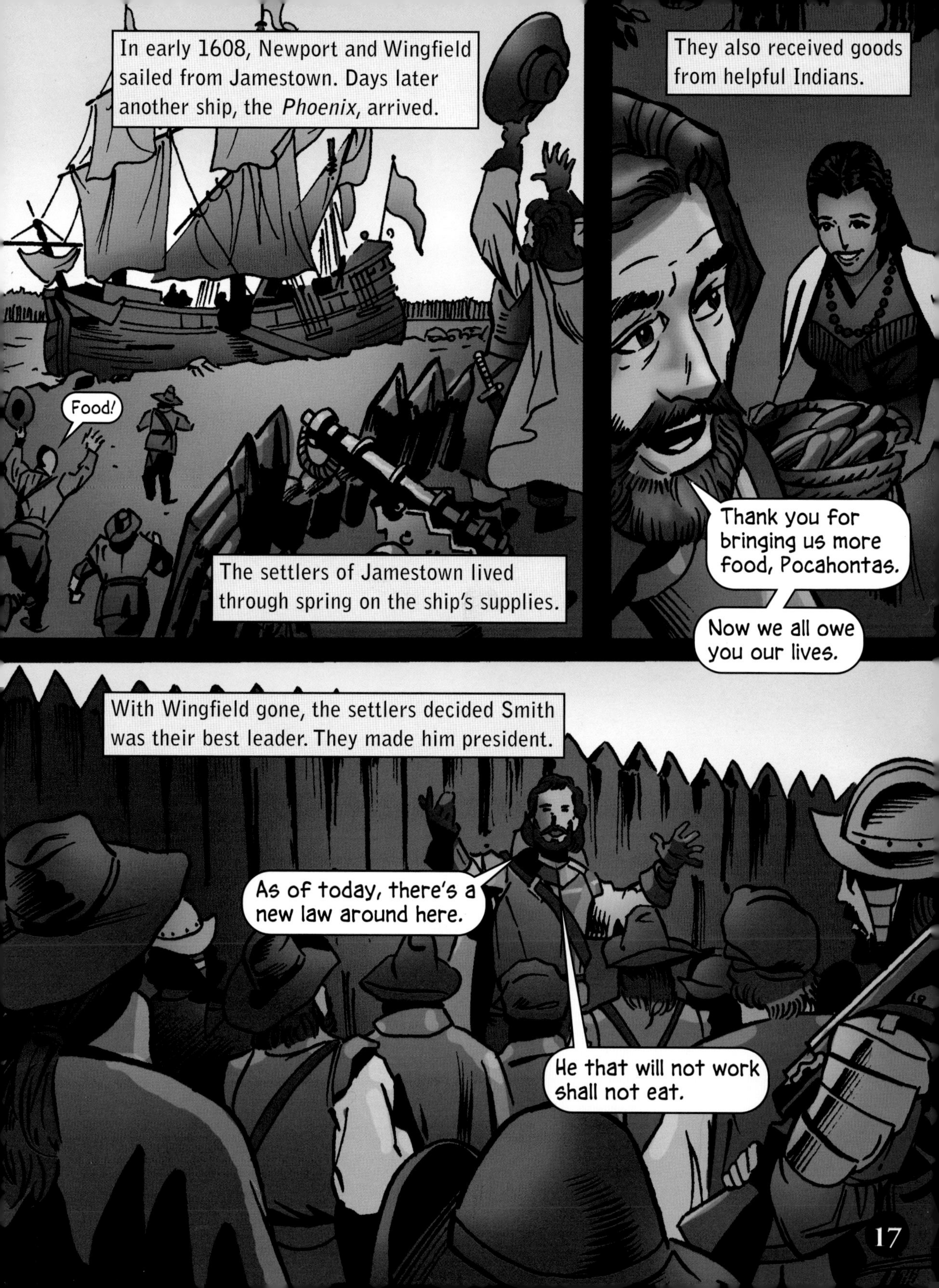
In early 1608, Newport and Wingfield sailed from Jamestown. Days later another ship, the *Phoenix*, arrived.
Food!
The settlers of Jamestown lived through spring on the ship's supplies.
They also received goods from helpful Indians.
Thank you for bringing us more food, Pocahontas.
Now we all owe you our lives.
With Wingfield gone, the settlers decided Smith was their best leader. They made him president.
As of today, there's a new law around here.
He that will not work shall not eat.

CHAPTER 3

A Struggle to Survive

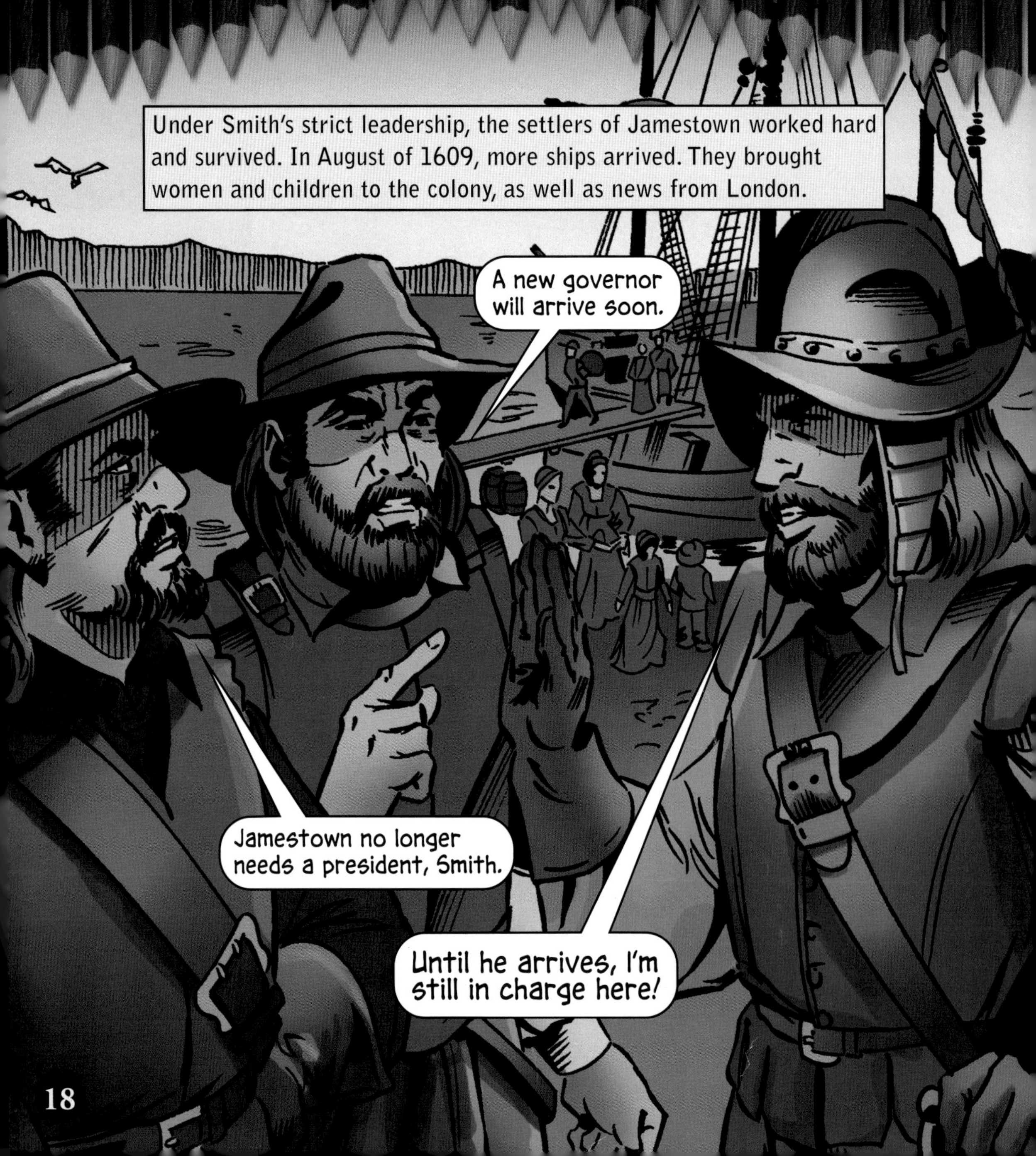

Under Smith's strict leadership, the settlers of Jamestown worked hard and survived. In August of 1609, more ships arrived. They brought women and children to the colony, as well as news from London.
A new governor will arrive soon.
Jamestown no longer needs a president, Smith.
Until he arrives, I'm still in charge here!

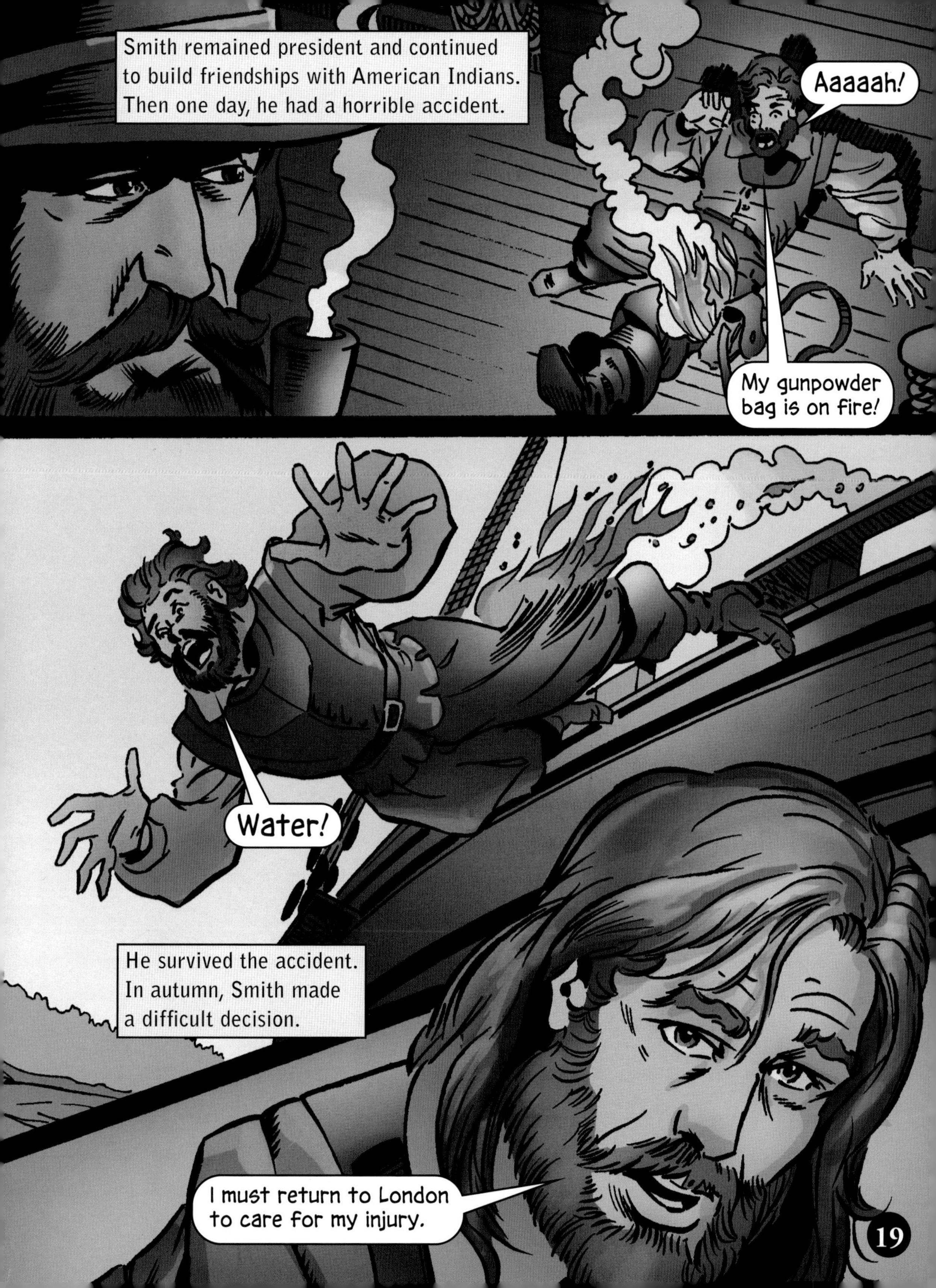
Smith remained president and continued to build friendships with American Indians. Then one day, he had a horrible accident.
Aaaaah!
My gunpowder bag is on fire!
Water!
He survived the accident. In autumn, Smith made a difficult decision.
I must return to London to care for my injury.

With Smith gone, Jamestown needed a leader. The settlers chose George Percy, an educated gentleman from a noble family.
We have at most three months of food left, President Percy.
And our fishing nets have rotted in the water.
Ratcliffe, tell this Powhatan to give us more food.
Percy's demands for food angered Powhatan. The chief sent men to attack the settlers.
They forced the settlers to stay inside the fort.
We're trapped!
What will we eat?
That winter became known as the "starving time."

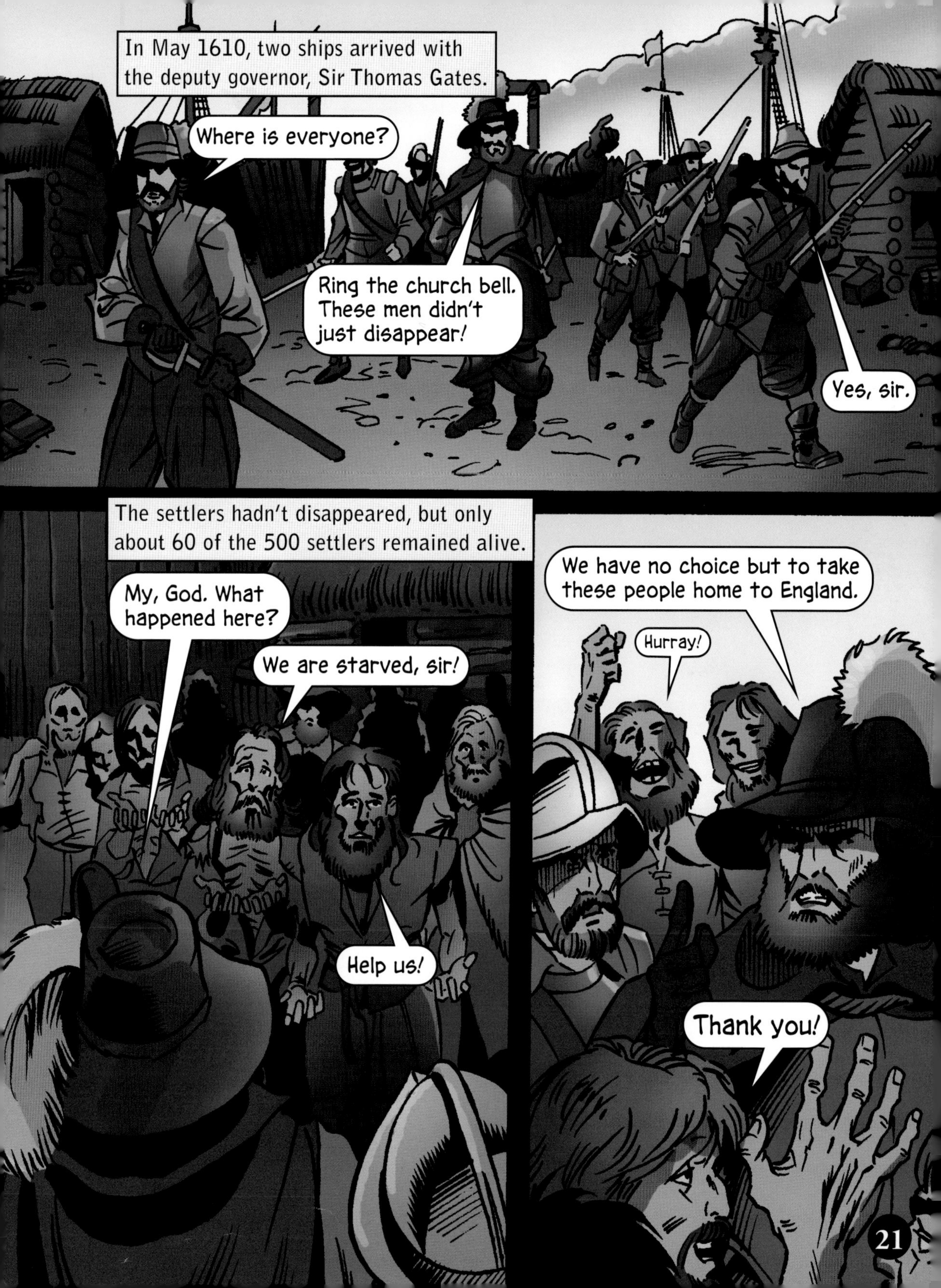
In May 1610, two ships arrived with the deputy governor, Sir Thomas Gates.
Where is everyone?
Ring the church bell. These men didn't just disappear!
Yes, sir.
The settlers hadn't disappeared, but only about 60 of the 500 settlers remained alive.
My, God. What happened here?
We are starved, sir!
Help us!
We have no choice but to take these people home to England.
Hurray!
Thank you!

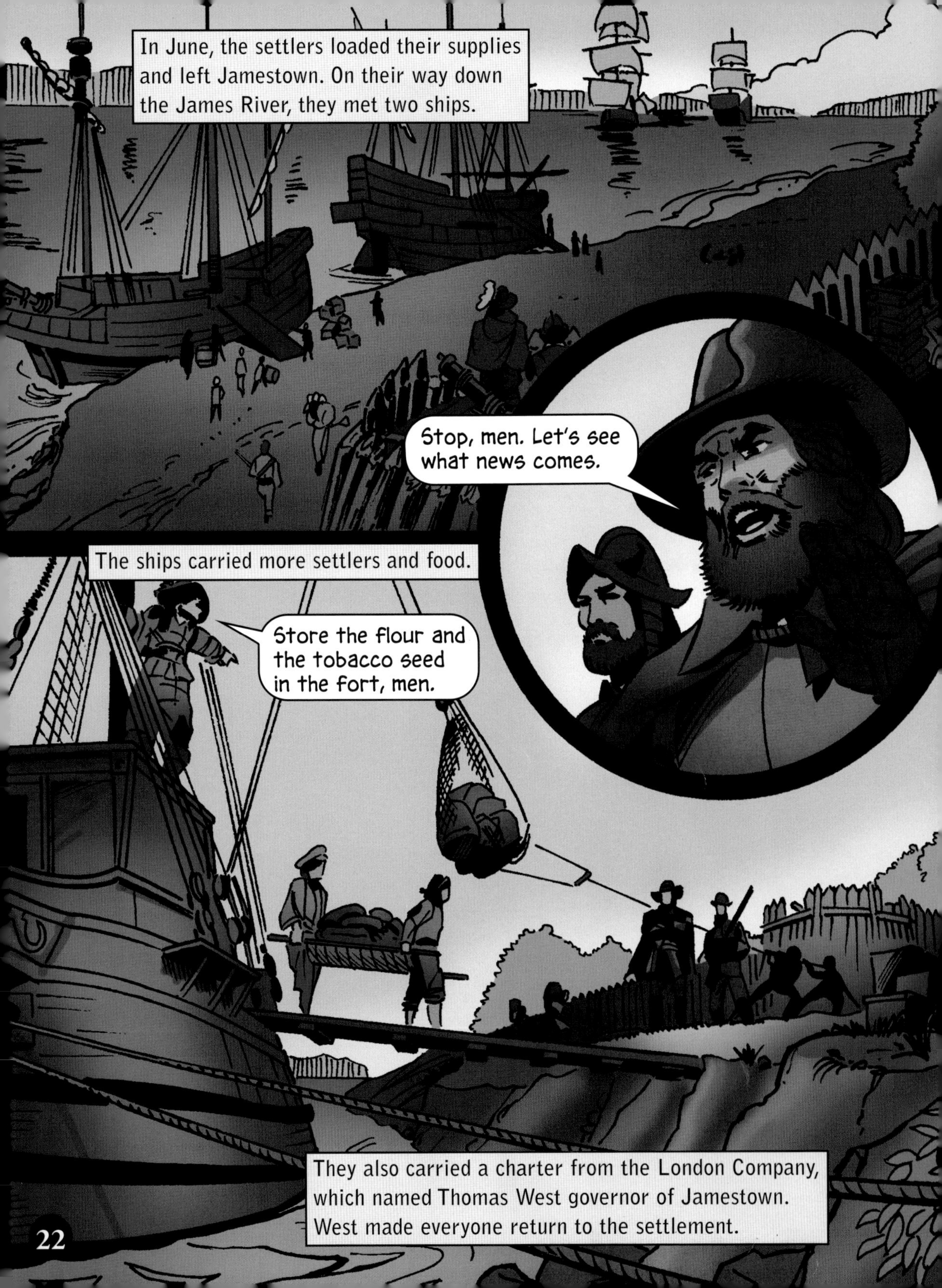
In June, the settlers loaded their supplies and left Jamestown. On their way down the James River, they met two ships.
Stop, men. Let's see what news comes.
The ships carried more settlers and food.
Store the flour and the tobacco seed in the fort, men.
They also carried a charter from the London Company, which named Thomas West governor of Jamestown. West made everyone return to the settlement.

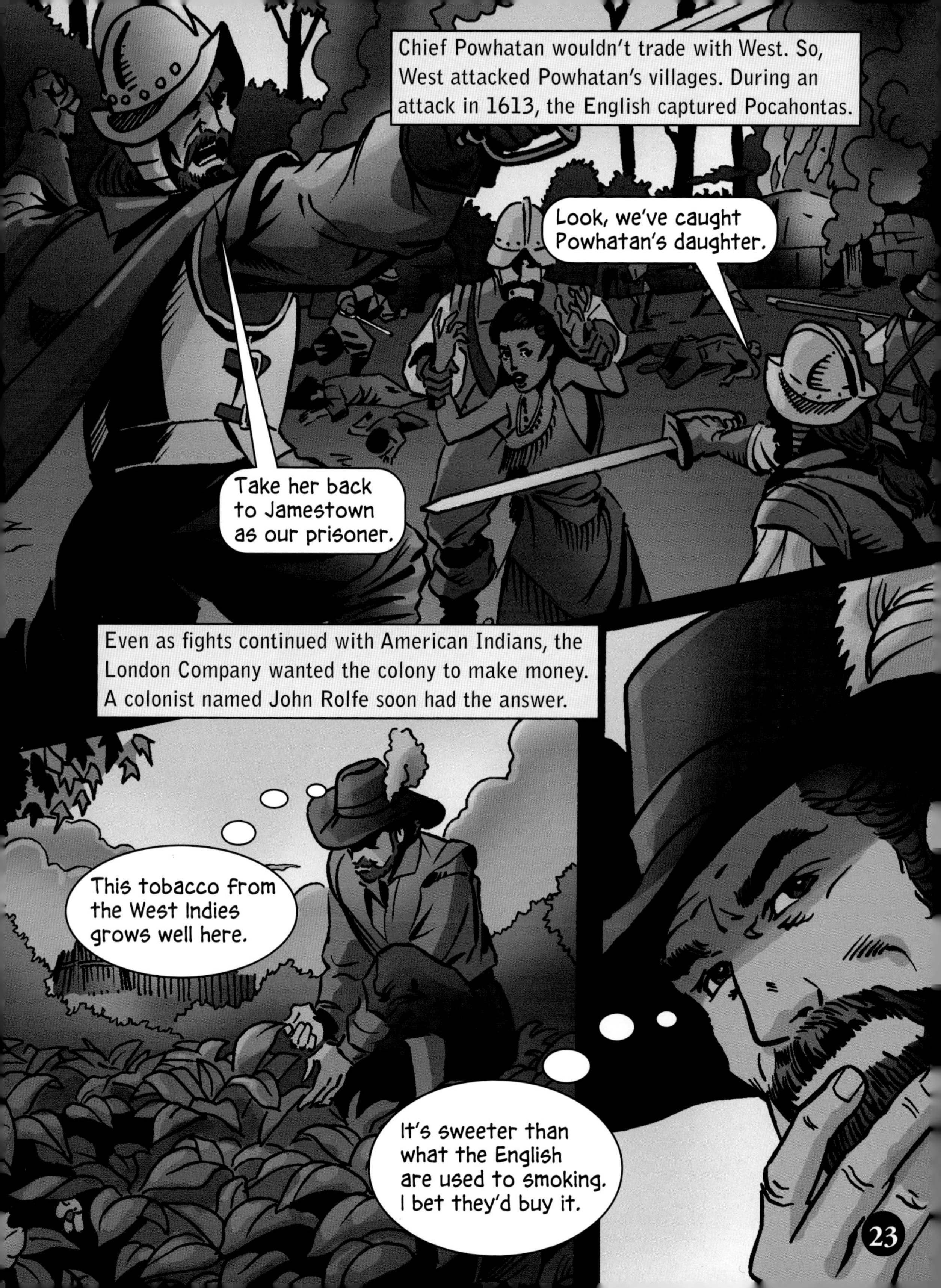
Chief Powhatan wouldn't trade with West. So, West attacked Powhatan's villages. During an attack in 1613, the English captured Pocahontas.
Look, we've caught Powhatan's daughter.
Take her back to Jamestown as our prisoner.
Even as fights continued with American Indians, the London Company wanted the colony to make money. A colonist named John Rolfe soon had the answer.
This tobacco from the West Indies grows well here.
It's sweeter than what the English are used to smoking. I bet they'd buy it.

CHAPTER 4

The End of Jamestown

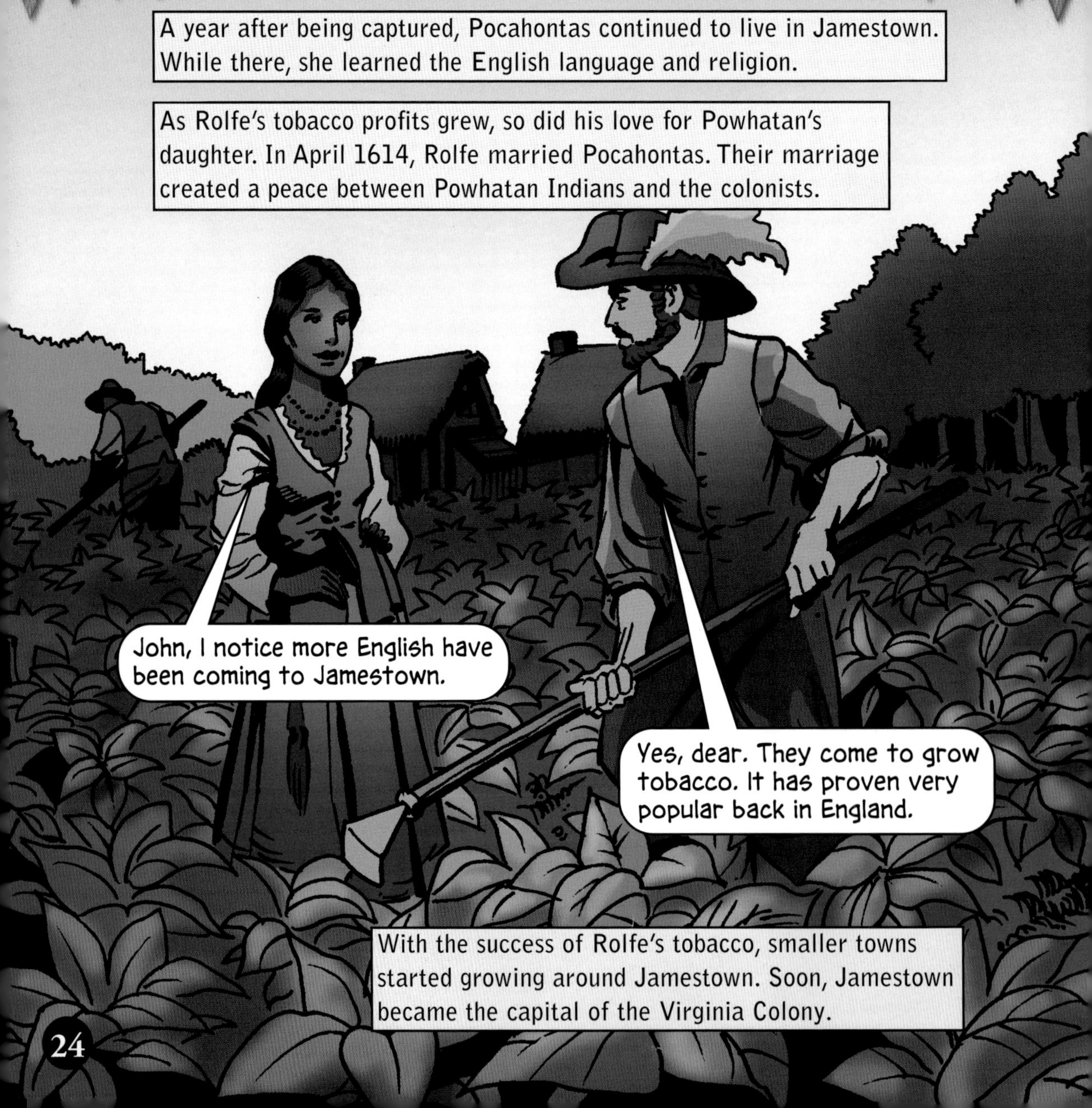
A year after being captured, Pocahontas continued to live in Jamestown. While there, she learned the English language and religion.
As Rolfe's tobacco profits grew, so did his love for Powhatan's daughter. In April 1614, Rolfe married Pocahontas. Their marriage created a peace between Powhatan Indians and the colonists.
John, I notice more English have been coming to Jamestown.
Yes, dear. They come to grow tobacco. It has proven very popular back in England.
With the success of Rolfe's tobacco, smaller towns started growing around Jamestown. Soon, Jamestown became the capital of the Virginia Colony.

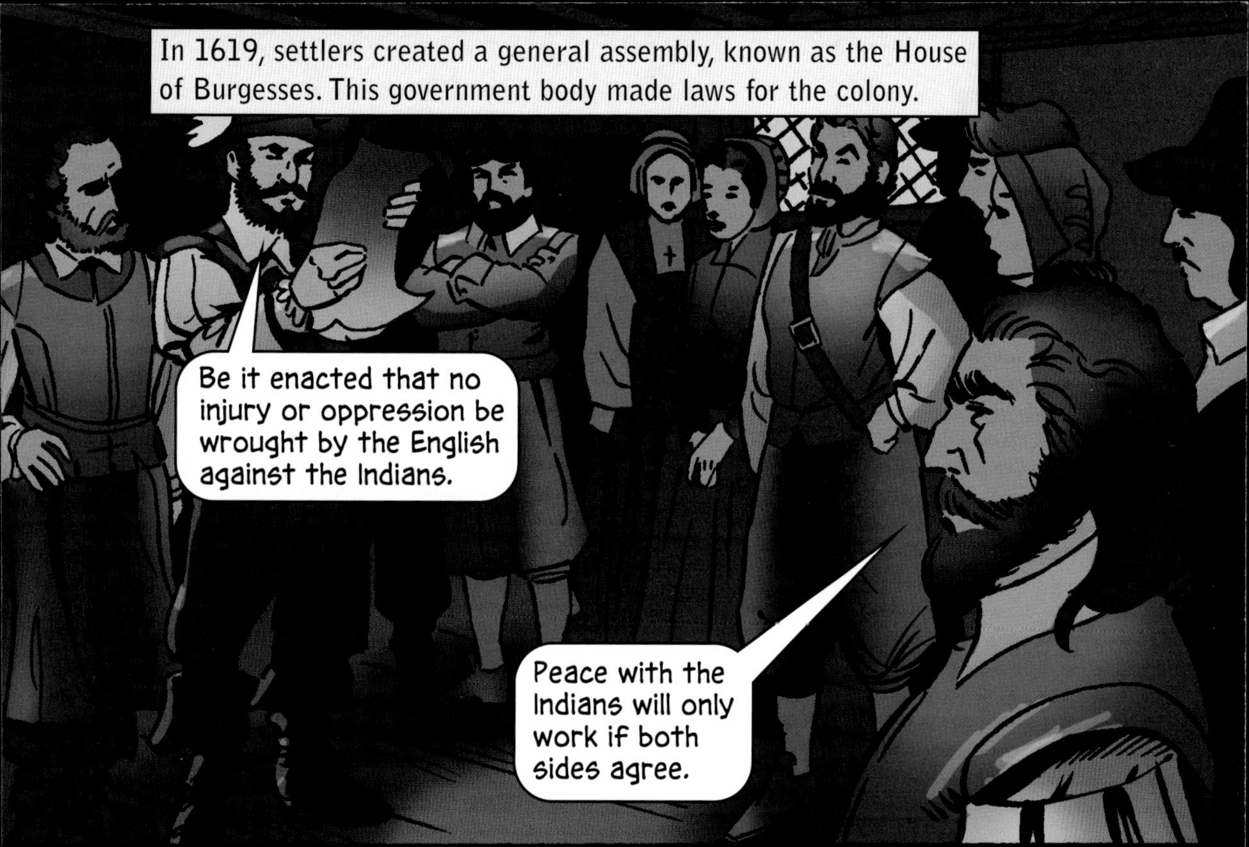
In 1619, settlers created a general assembly, known as the House of Burgesses. This government body made laws for the colony.
Be it enacted that no injury or oppression be wrought by the English against the Indians.
Peace with the Indians will only work if both sides agree.

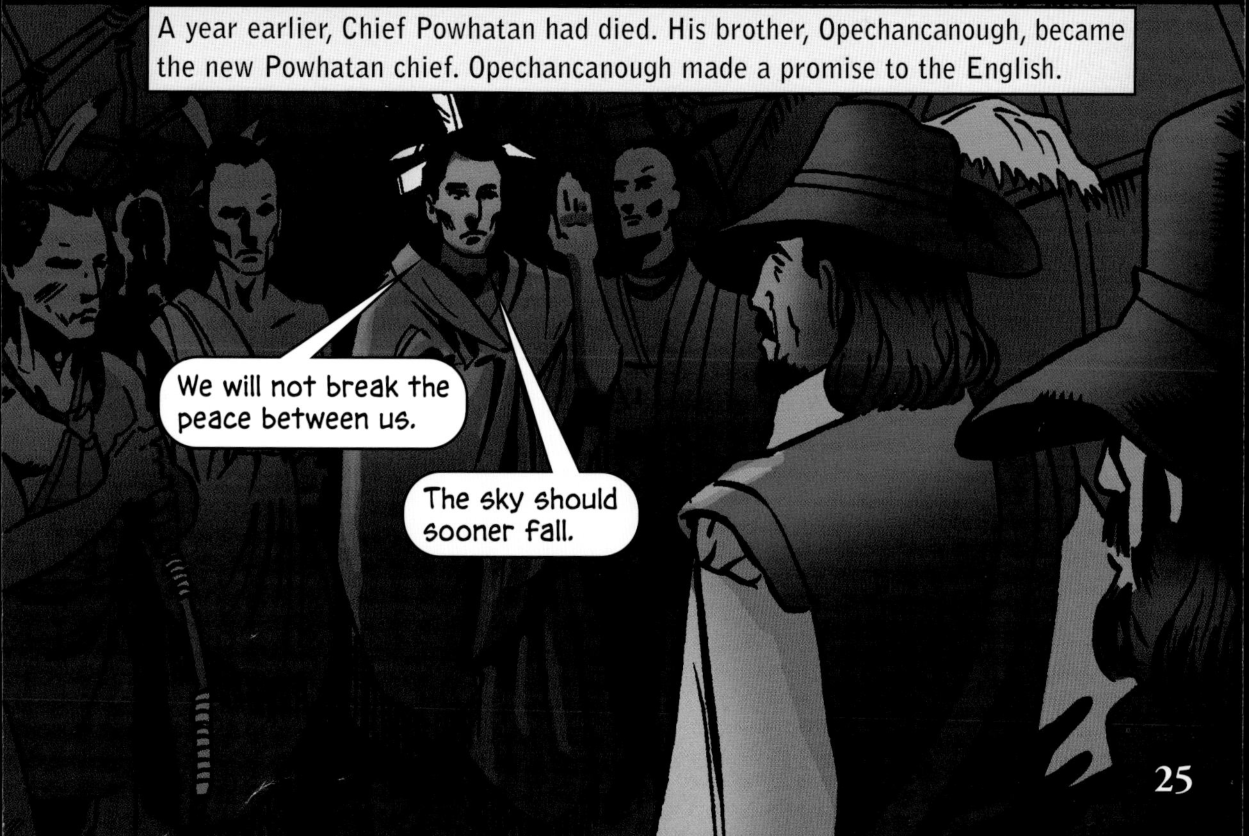
A year earlier, Chief Powhatan had died. His brother, Opechancanough, became the new Powhatan chief. Opechancanough made a promise to the English.
We will not break the peace between us.
The sky should sooner fall.

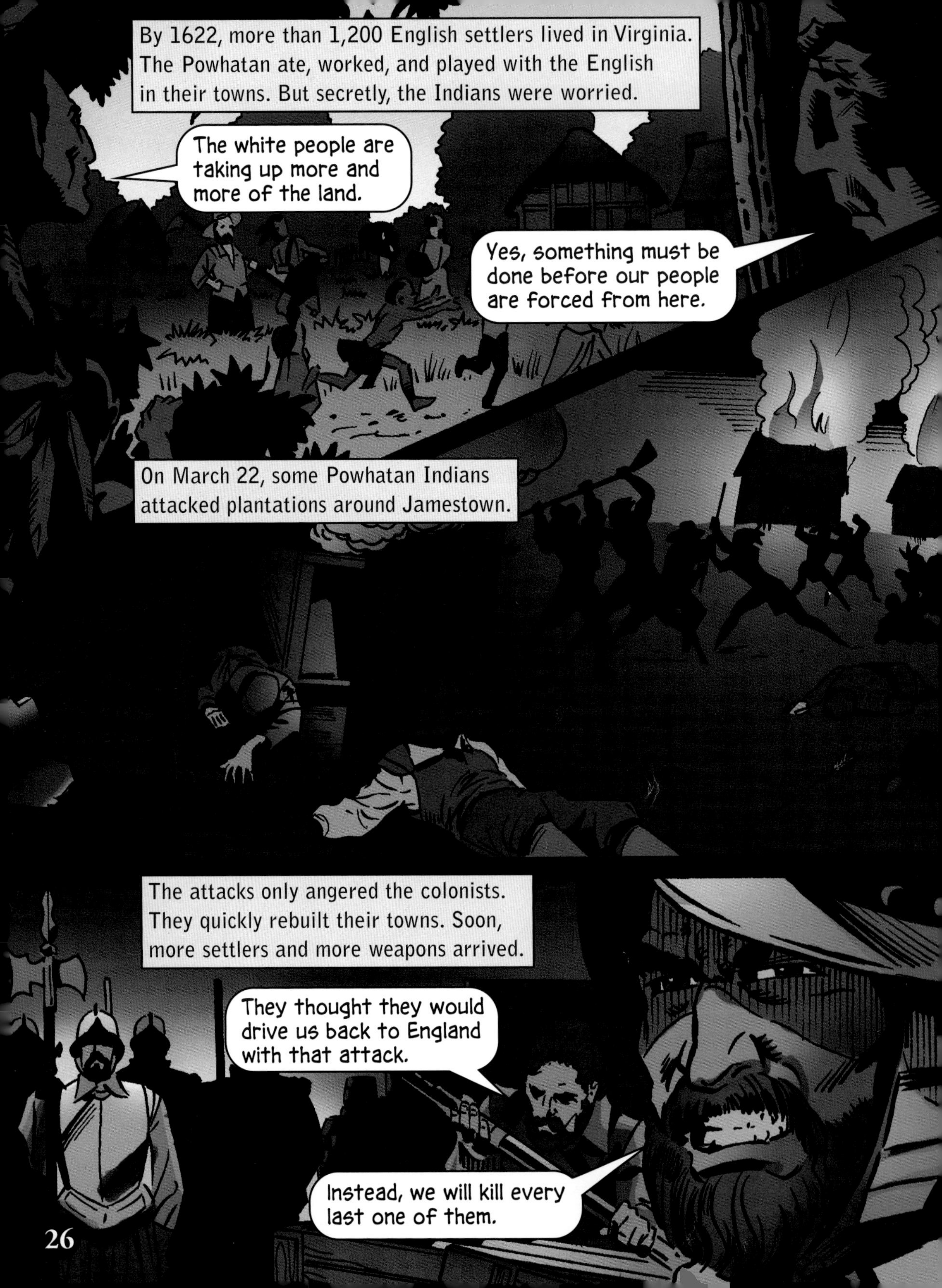
By 1622, more than 1,200 English settlers lived in Virginia. The Powhatan ate, worked, and played with the English in their towns. But secretly, the Indians were worried.
The white people are taking up more and more of the land.
Yes, something must be done before our people are forced from here.
On March 22, some Powhatan Indians attacked plantations around Jamestown.
The attacks only angered the colonists. They quickly rebuilt their towns. Soon, more settlers and more weapons arrived.
They thought they would drive us back to England with that attack.
Instead, we will kill every last one of them.

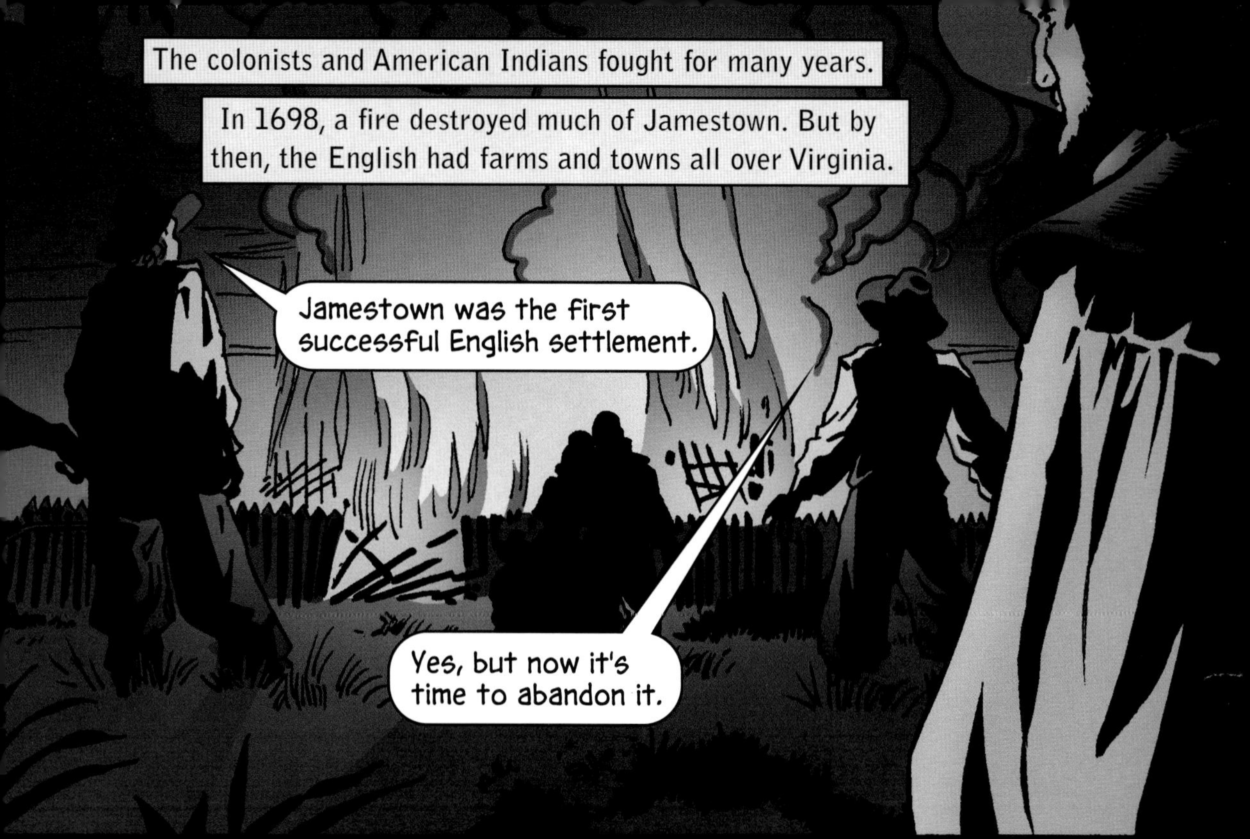
The colonists and American Indians fought for many years.
In 1698, a fire destroyed much of Jamestown. But by then, the English had farms and towns all over Virginia.
Jamestown was the first successful English settlement.
Yes, but now it's time to abandon it.

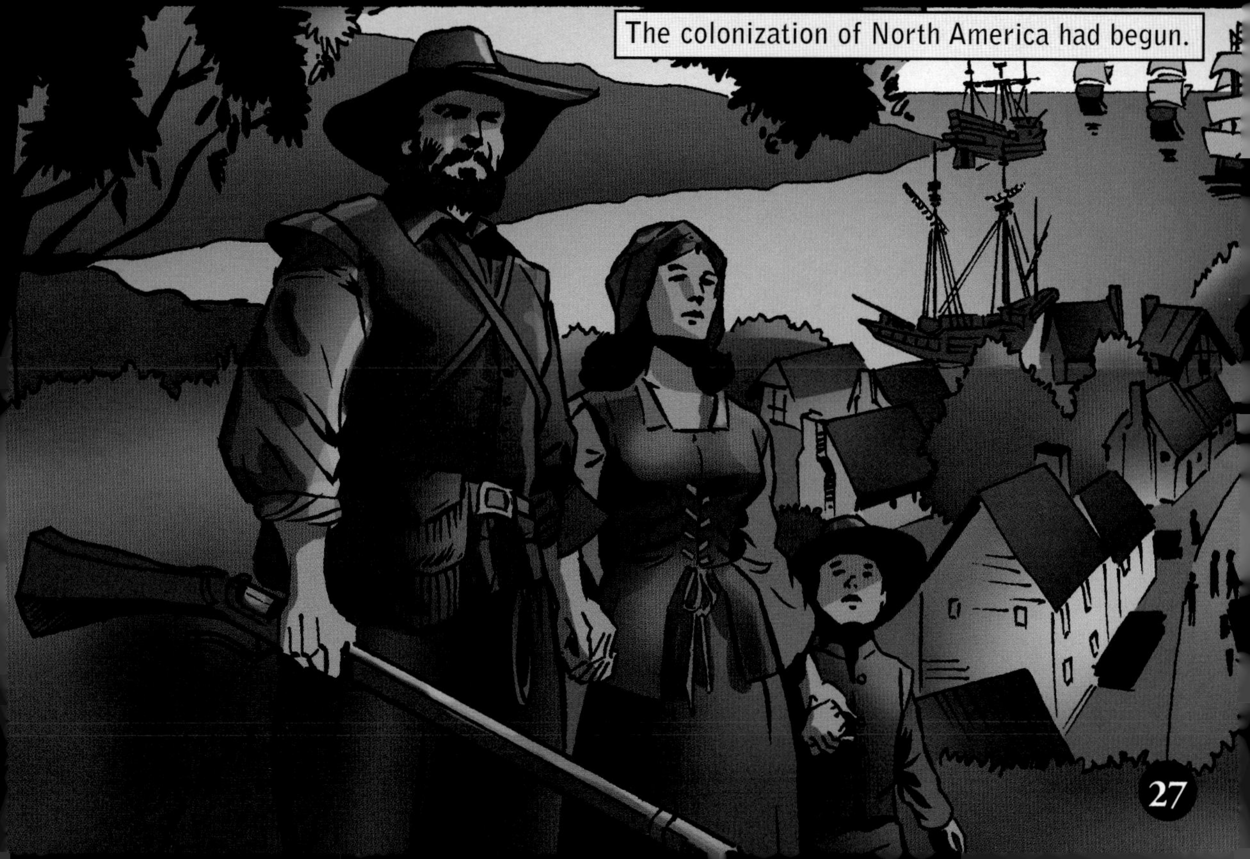
The colonization of North America had begun.

MORE ABOUT

Jamestown

✳ Jamestown is known as the first permanent English settlement in North America. But more than 30 years earlier, Englishmen settled on Roanoke Island, off the North Carolina coast. Today, Roanoke is called the Lost Colony. No one knows what happened to these settlers.

✳ In 1616, John Rolfe, Pocahontas, and their baby traveled to London. Less than a year later, Pocahontas died at the age of 22. Some historians believe she died of pneumonia or tuberculosis caused by the city's foul, smoky air.

✳ After returning to England, Captain John Smith recovered from his injury. Smith never returned to Jamestown. But in April 1614, he traveled to the areas of Maine and Massachusetts Bay. Smith named this region New England.

✳ In 1624, Smith wrote a book about his experiences at Jamestown. In the book, Smith claims that Pocahontas saved him from being killed by Chief Powhatan. Most historians believe Powhatan never wanted to kill Smith. Instead, they think either Pocahontas was performing an American Indian ceremony, or Smith made up the story.

* In August 1619, the first Africans came to North America aboard a Dutch ship. The 20 or so men were sold in Jamestown for food and supplies. Eventually, thousands of other Africans would be shipped to America as slaves.

* In 1676, a young planter named Nathaniel Bacon led a revolt against Jamestown's governor, William Berkeley. Bacon believed Berkeley could have stopped Indian attacks on settlements west of Jamestown. During what is known as Bacon's Rebellion, most of Jamestown burned to the ground.

* In 1994, archaeologists from the Association for Preservation of Virginia Antiquities (APVA) started digging in the area of Jamestown. They found two of the three walls from the fort. They also found thousands of artifacts from the time of the first settlers. Today, the area of Jamestown is a national historic site.

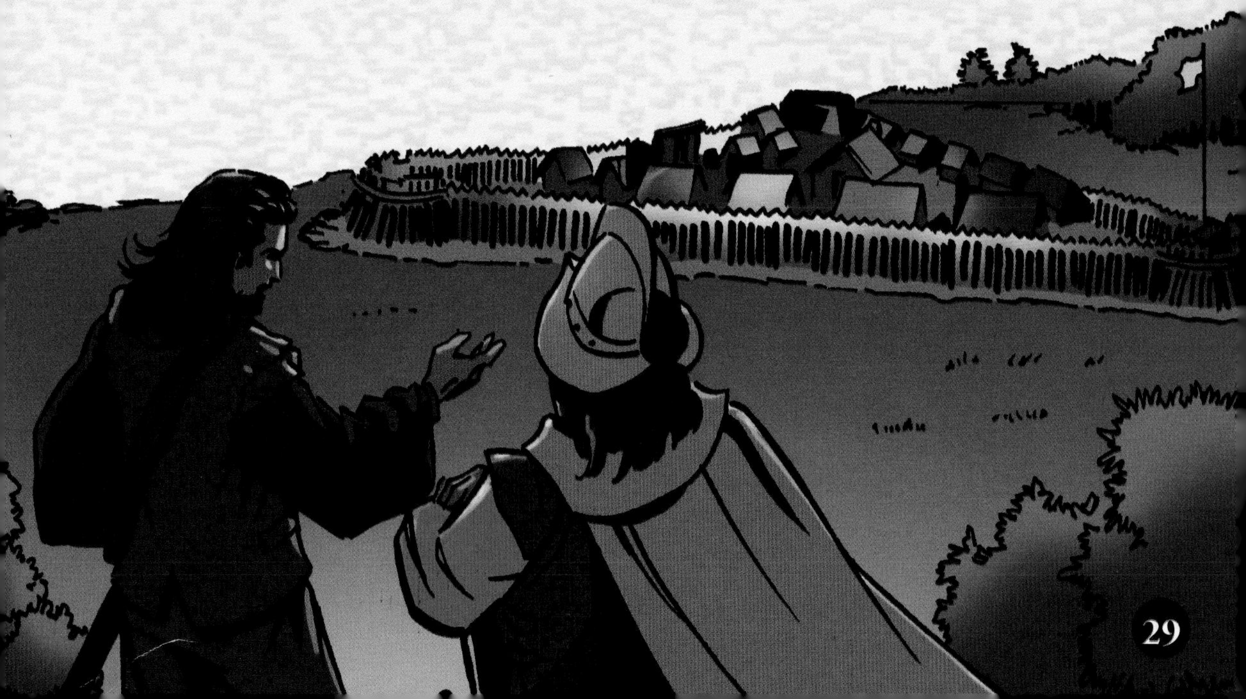

GLOSSARY

archaeologist (ar-kee-OL-uh-jist)—a scientist who studies objects from long ago

artifact (ART-uh-fakt)—an object made by human beings, especially a tool or weapon used in the past

charter (CHAR-tur)—a formal document that states the duties and rights of a group of people

confederacy (kuhn-FED-ur-uh-see)—a union of groups; Powhatan groups united under one government called the Powhatan Confederacy.

territory (TER-uh-tor-ee)—a large area of land

INTERNET SITES

FactHound offers a safe, fun way to find Internet sites related to this book. All of the sites on FactHound have been researched by our staff.

Here's how:

1. Visit *www.facthound.com*
2. Type in this special code **073684967X** for age-appropriate sites. Or enter a search word related to this book for a more general search.
3. Click on the **Fetch It** button.

FactHound will fetch the best sites for you!

READ MORE

Doak, Robin S. *Smith: John Smith and the Settlement of Jamestown*. Exploring the World. Minneapolis: Compass Point Books, 2003.

Riehecky, Janet. *The Settling of Jamestown*. Landmark Events in American History. Milwaukee: World Almanac Library, 2002.

Sonneborn, Liz. *Pocahontas, 1595–1617*. American Indian Biographies. Mankato, Minn.: Blue Earth Books, 2003.

BIBLIOGRAPHY

Barbour, Philip L. *Pocahontas and Her World*. Boston: Houghton Mifflin, 1970.

Bridenbaugh, Carl. *Jamestown: 1544–1699*. New York: Oxford University Press, 1980.

Price, David A. *Love and Hate in Jamestown: John Smith, Pocahontas, and the Heart of a New Nation*. New York: Knopf, 2003.

Rountree, Helen C. *Pocahontas, Powhatan, Opechancanough: Three Indian Lives Changed by Jamestown*. Charlottesville: University of Virginia Press, 2005.

INDEX